CAMRA'S
Peak District
Pub Walks

CAMRA'S
Peak District

Pub Walks

BOB STEEL

Published by the Campaign for Real Ale
230 Hatfield Road
St Albans
Hertfordshire AL1 4LW

www.camra.org.uk/books

© Campaign for Real Ale 2008

First published 2008
Reprinted with corrections 2010

ISBN 978-1-85249-246-5

A CIP catalogue record for this book is
available from the British Library

Printed and bound in Singapore by
NPE Print Communications Pte Ltd

Managing Editor: **Simon Hall**

Project Editor: **Emma Haines**

Copy Editor: **Hugh Thompson**

Editorial Assistance: **Katie Hunt**

Design/Typography: **Stephen Bere (bluebeetle design)**

Cover Design: **Dale Tomlinson**

Marketing Manager: **Kim Carvey**

Ordnance Survey mapping: **the National Map Centre, St Albans**

Maps: John Plumer **(JP Map Graphics Ltd)**

Photographs: **Bob Steel**

Additional photographs: **www.visitpeakdistrict.com**
(pp. 2-3, 9, 10, 13-15, 17, 18, 31, 32, 53, 54, 72, 85, 86, 96,
105, 117, 118, 132) ; **Thornbridge Brewery** (pp.11)

Additional cover photography: **Gettyimages/Peter Cade**

Index: **Hilary Bird**

Contents

How to use this guide

The walks in this guide have been grouped around the larger towns in the Peak District area, all of which make suitable bases for a foray into the National Park. The walks are suitable for day trippers to the Peak, or you could combine several of the routes for a longer walking holiday.

Overview map

This map can be found on page 16. It shows the locations of all the walks and is useful when planning a longer trip that takes in several of the walks, or organising transport and accommodation. Accommodation and transport information can be found on pages 146-150.

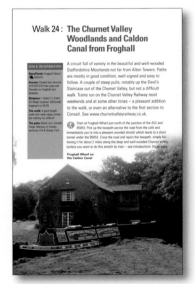

KEY FOR WALK MAPS

    Walk start point

■ ■   Walk route

• • • •   Detour

    Featured pub

A   Corresponds to grid reference in the text

➤   Direction of walk

    Ordnance Survey grid reference

Walk information

Located on first page of each walk, this tinted box will give you some general information needed to plan your route including the start point, public transport access, distance and pubs worth visiting. Further information about the walk such as terrain and suggested start time can often be found in the opening paragraph.

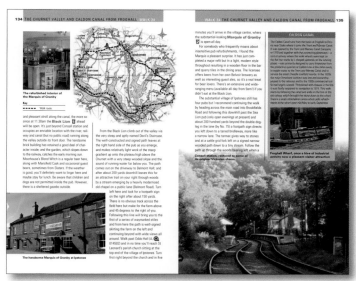

Mapping

The routes are plotted on Ordnance Survey maps, with suggested detours clearly marked. The start (⊙), waypoints (Ⓐ) and featured pubs (🔟) are marked on the map as shown.

The routes

Featured pubs are numbered as they appear in the route and written in red. Other recommended pubs are written in italics. Ordnance Survey grid references are marked with a (⊙) symbol, and those grid references shown on the map labelled with the corresponding letter (waypoints).

Information boxes

Tinted boxes give you information about local history, geography and other features of note.

Pub information

A tinted box at the end of each walk gives you information about the pubs featured in the route, with information such as the opening hours, contact details and the times that food is served – it is recommended that you phone ahead to check times with the pubs, as these can be subject to change. The numbers correspond with those in the text and on the map. This box also includes information about other recommended pubs and nearby attractions.

Introduction

Welcome to CAMRA's Peak District Pub Walks. My first trip to this area was as a student in the 1970s, and I have been a regular admirer since. This book is a celebration of the landscape as well as of the fine pubs that are still to be found.

Choosing the pubs

When it came to choosing the pubs for this guide there were a few criteria that were imperative to its success. Firstly, and most importantly, the pubs have to offer traditional cask ale in excellent condition. CAMRA also looks for welcoming pubs with good facilities and atmosphere, as well as celebrating those with tasty food, pleasant accommodation and ones that are family-friendly. I have avoided including establishments where the drinker, as opposed to the diner, is sidelined or made to feel unwelcome. We seek to celebrate the traditional values of the pub: good beer, a welcome to all and comfortable but unpretentious surroundings.

No other guide to the Peak District tells you as much about the beer quality and range available. All pubs in this guide are here with the agreement of local branches of the Campaign for Real Ale, and this is your best assurance of a great pint.

Peak District signage

The walks

The walks are arranged in groups to suit the beer tourist who might be visiting for a weekend or longer. Each of the eight umbrella locations would make good bases for these longer stays: most are larger settlements with plenty of accommodation options; but additionally each route carries some accommodation suggestions of its own – see pp146–9.

The terrain

The terrain can be quite hilly. You ought to have a fair level of fitness before attempting

the walks; and remember post-pub distances before overindulging, especially if you have some mileage to cover! We have avoided simplistic grading systems for difficulty of the routes in favour of a descriptive assessment of the degree of challenge on the route including the ease of navigation. In fact the great majority of the routes are easy to follow thanks to the generally excellent signage of paths and rights of way in and around the Peak District National Park.

Public transport

By the standards of rural areas, the Peak District is still well provided for as regards public transport, thanks in large part to a generous subsidy for local authorities. Even if you arrive in the Peak by car you should be able to make good use of local bus services. And, of course, using buses and trains (and taxis where this is not possible) makes good sense if you are enjoying a drink in the region's pubs. If you have bought this book I would strongly recommend as an indispensable companion the inexpensive *Peak District Bus Timetable* produced and regularly updated by Derbyshire County Council. It's available at tourist information centers and other outlets for next to nothing. Another valuable resource is the excellent Traveline web site at www.traveline.org.uk, which has a regional journey planner facility.

Peak pubs

Like everywhere else, pubs here have closed in large numbers in the past – although the trend has slowed somewhat recently as tourism has grown. This has put its own pressures on pubs

right **Walking along Curbar Edge, White Peak**

and the traditional, unfussy local is increasingly hard to find; this guide will help you find them. This is because, as with my *London Pub Walks*, one of its aims is to celebrate those pubs which have survived insensitive modernisation and alteration sufficiently to be included on CAMRA's National or (draft) Regional Inventory of notable pub interiors. Find out more at www.heritagepubs.org.uk.

If you are interested in the history and lore of pubs in the region I can thoroughly recommend Andrew McCloy's *Peakland Pubs* (Halsgrove Press), a well-written and engaging read which unearths some fascinating tales about the history of the locals in this region. Also recommended is the Ordnance Survey map for the area of the walk. The relevant sheet(s) are given at the start of each walk.

Opening times

These are correct at the time of going to press but it is advisable to check, particularly for lunchtime hours: in general a lot of Peakland pubs do not open on weekday lunchtimes or they may be shut on some days – Monday lunchtime is a bad time, for example. Also, if you're aiming to arrive at a pub for lunch, consider the length of the morning walk and a suitable start time: advice is given regarding this, and some routes can be reversed to lengthen or shorten the morning or afternoon sections.

Children and animals

Many pubs in the Peak welcome children, perhaps in the dining room or in general before the late evening session. Information is given under many of the entries, but if in doubt it is wise to ring ahead. Equally, if you're walking with a dog, it is always as well to check the current state of affairs with any pub you are intending to visit.

Towards a greener pint

One welcome development of the rise of microbreweries is the prospect of reducing beer miles by buying local. A shining example is the Charles Cotton at Hartington, which has five cask ales all sourced from local micros by direct delivery. A version of the successful 'Locale' scheme initiated by the Nottingham branch of CAMRA may be rolled out nationally during the currency of this guide but in the meantime you can encourage this welcome development by asking for directly delivered local beers.

Peak District pub walks on the internet

There is a forum online for owners of this book to share their experiences of the routes in the book – the walks themselves, the beer quality, suggestions for additions/deletions etc. Visit www.aletrails.com and follow the links to Peak District Pub Walks.

Walking in the unique Peakland landscape

The Peak District pub and brewery scene

Much has changed since I first started visiting the Peak some thirty years ago. Then the National Park was served beer-wise by the large regional brewers such as Marstons, Wards and Robinsons, whilst Nottingham brewers Home, Shipstones and Hardy Hansons also had outlets in the Park. These latter three have all disappeared, of course, but here, as elsewhere, the theme has been the rise of microbreweries. Indeed, the region is very well endowed with local breweries who have now seized a sizeable share of the market for real ale within and around the National Park – the 2008 *Good Beer Guide* lists over twenty of them within Derbyshire alone!

> 'Nay, I am for the country liquor, Derbyshire ale, if you please; for a man should not, methinks, come from London to drink wine in the Peak'
>
> *The Compleat Angler* by Isaac Walton

Some of these come and go but a number of them have already won awards at CAMRA and other events, and look set to play a significant part in the local real ale scene for a long time to come. Thornbridge Brewery near Bakewell is one example. Established in 2005, they have already picked up nearly 50 awards from CAMRA and the Small Independent Brewers' Association (SIBA) at their festivals, especially for their strong IPA, Jaipur. They have succeeded in securing a good number of outlets for their beers in the regional trade proving that there is room for new good quality products despite the apparent wall-to-wall domination of the bland national and international brewers. Users of this book will notice that a good range of well-kept ales is now available in many of the pubs featured although, as in many tourist-oriented regions, that range may be reduced in winter in order that quality is maintained – it's important to maintain a brisk turnover of cask ale to keep quality high!

Another change since the seventies is in the availability and quality of food on offer in pubs. Whilst your scribe doesn't approve of pubs which have been turned into restaurants and, by and large, such establishments do not feature within, the days of food being limited to the odd pork pie and a clingfilm wrapped roll have thankfully passed into history. You'll definitely be able to eat well using this guide, in pubs that are happy to see you if you 'only' want to drink whilst offering good quality food in a pubby atmosphere.

What's also noticeable is that a good proportion of the pubs I knew as a young man have remained relatively 'unspoilt by progress', to borrow a phrase from a well known regional brewer. Maybe this is due to the large numbers of walkers and cyclists who visit the region and are happy with a simple environment where muddy boots and outdoor togs are still welcome. There have been some spectacular casualties in this regard and some gruesome passing fads – I remember several pubs in the peak being rebadged with names from Tolkein (The Prancing Pony at Foolow and the Hobbit at Monyash come to mind). Mercifully these inns have now reverted to their former names – the Bull's Head in both cases. Long may they remain that way. Readers who appreciate simple unspoilt pubs should consult the section on historic pub interiors on page 12.

The award-winning Thornbridge Brewery

left: **Quiet Woman, Earl Sterndale** centre: **Duke of York, Elton** right: **Holly Bush Inn, Makeney**

Historic pub interiors

The pub is one of the great British traditions, stretching back into antiquity and reinforced by pub signs such as 'Ye Olde…' etc. Ironically, despite such appeals to history, few pub interiors have much claim to antiquity, since not many have survived the last fifty years without major alteration.

Defending Britain's traditional pubs, as well as its traditional beers, has always been one of CAMRA's declared concerns. By the early 1980s, when the Campaign set up its Pub Preservation Group, it had become apparent that the nation's pub heritage was under severe threat yet was largely ignored by mainstream conservation bodies. Change in pubs has always occurred, and has reflected developments in society; but since the 1960s and 1970s in particular, the British pub has been subject to an accelerated and often destructive wave of internal alterations. In rural areas, such as the Peak District, these changes have often taken the form of opening up the building with extensions to include kitchens and supposedly making the place more appealing to the affluent car-borne tourist.

The relationship to statutory listing

Some readers will be aware that in the United Kingdom many buildings are statutorily 'listed'. This means they meet strict national criteria of 'architectural or historic interest.' The weakness of the listing process is that until very recently it has concentrated primarily upon architectural quality or significance, with little or no reference to the things that make a pub a pub. However, many of our most unspoilt pubs have no architectural pretensions at all – the simple rural beerhouses like the Duke of York at Elton for example. This sort of pub has been the biggest casualty in the relentless modernisation process and has been largely unprotected by listing.

CAMRA's inventories of historic pub interiors

CAMRA's concern about the fate of authentic historic pub interiors met with strong support from English Heritage, and the CAMRA National Inventory (NI) was born. It identifies pubs that retain the most complete and important historic interiors in the country. Its sole concern is with the internal physical fabric of those pubs in terms of historical intactness and rarity value. As a result of this project, several previously unvalued gems have been uncovered, and a number of valuable interiors have been given listed status.

Sadly, very few Peakland pubs make it into the National Inventory or 'Premier Division' of pub interiors. The best of them, however, like the Barley Mow at Kirk Ireton (Walk 2), the Three Stags' Heads at Wardlow Mires (Walk 10) and the Duke of York, Elton (Walk 11) are featured, and all serve fine cask ale.

Several other pubs, although altered, still retain enough of historic interest to be regarded as of regional significance. CAMRA has a draft database of these pubs on a Regional Inventory (RI) which, like the NI, is very much a work in progress. Among the best of these featured in this book are the Quiet Woman, Earl Sterndale (Walk 21) (which your author considers a candidate for promotion!); the Flying Childers, Stanton-in-Peak (Walk 9), the Bell, Cromford (Walks 4 & 6) and the Holly Bush, Makeney (Walk 1).

As mentioned elsewhere, readers interested in the heritage and history of Peak pubs are recommended to consult Andrew McCloy's book, *Peakland Pubs*, published by Halsgrove in 2005.

With thanks to Geoff Brandwood (co-author of Licensed to Sell: The History and Heritage of the Public House *published by English Heritage in 2004).*

Safety first!

The countryside code

When walking in the Peak District, or anywhere else in the countryside, it's always worth following a few simple, common-sense guidelines to help protect the countryside that you're enjoying and keep you safe.

- Plan ahead and be prepared for the unexpected. Bad weather and restricted access to land – for example, during breeding season – may force you to alter you plans, so follow local signs and advice and don't be afraid to turn back.
- Leave gates as you find them. The countryside is a working area and even well-intentioned actions can affect people's livelihoods and the welfare of animals.
- Protect the appearance, flora and fauna of the Peak District by taking your litter home.
- If you're walking with a dog, keep it under control. It's your responsibility to make sure your dog is not a nuisance or a danger to farm animals, wildlife or other people.
- Consider other people – other walkers, riders and cyclists and those who work and live in the countryside.

What to wear and what to take

Many readers will be experienced walkers and may not need any advice, but if you're relatively new to walking the following tips may be useful. The walks in this book do not venture into remote country and habitation and roads are always close by, but nonetheless you should be well equipped for comfort as well as safety.

Trainers or walking shoes with good grip are fine, but walking boots are recommended for more demanding terrain. They provide support for your ankles, which is useful when tackling steep slopes, and keep your feet warm and dry. A thick pair of socks will make them more comfortable in cold weather too.

Always pack enough clothing to wear for any potential turn in the weather. It's a good idea to have layers of clothes so that you can take one off or put one on as you warm up or the weather cools down. A waterproof jacket will keep off

A map is important if you're going to go exploring in the Peak

both rain and wind, with hoods and pockets being particularly useful features. Fleeces are good to wear in between your 'base layer' and jacket, especially ones with zips as they allow you to cool off easily if necessary. Avoid jeans – they take a long time to dry if they get wet. Lightweight, loose-fitting trousers made from synthetic material are favoured by walkers. They dry quickly and have handy pockets for carrying maps. Waterproof over-trousers or gaiters will prevent trousers and socks from getting wet, but can be difficult to get on and off easily.

Wear sun hats and sun cream in summer, if need be, and take plenty of water to drink. It's a good idea to carry something to eat – even if it's only a couple of cereal bars.

A rucksack can be very useful – use it to carry any spare clothing and food as well as other essentials like a map, compass, mobile phone, emergency whistle, torch, and simple first aid kit.

The maps and directions in this book will help you follow the walks, but if you want to venture off the beaten track to do a little more exploring on your own, or even connect sections of different walks from the book, a map and compass are invaluable – provided you know how to use them. Each walk lists the relevant Ordnance Survey Map in its introduction, as well as grid reference points along the route.

Cycling

Along with a vast network of footpaths, The Peak District is also home to a range of cycle-friendly bridleways and long-distance cycle trails. Three of these – the High Peak Trail, the Tissington Trail and the Manifold Track – follow the paths of disused railways and are detailed in a cycling section (p141) which also directs you to pubs and watering holes along the routes. Cyclists intending to sample some of the recommended brews should note that it is an offence to ride a bicycle on a road or other public place whilst unfit through drink to do so.

When cycling it is important to be both visible and safe. The cycling section includes details of cycle hire centres, all of which supply helmets and high-visibility reflectors, as well as bikes.

Saftey on the roads

Some of the routes include short stretches on rural lanes and roads. In general these are not very busy, but always take care as sometimes vehicles appear suddenly and travel quickly (especially on country roads with national speed limits). If there is not a footpath, walk in single file on the right-hand side (facing the traffic) except on corners and bends with poor visibility when you should cross (carefully) to get a better view. If you are using the section of the book on cycling, please remember that most of the pubs recommended lie away from the traffic-free trails; you'll need to access them using country lanes and roads. Cycle hire facilities are available and if in doubt you should seek advice there about the routes if you are lacking confidence about cycling in traffic.

Public transport

If relying on public transport, it is always worth checking the time of the last train or bus back to where you are staying before setting out on your day's walk, and noting down the number of a local taxi firm should you get into difficulties.

GLOSSARY	
Access land – areas that walkers have a right of access to	**Gritstone** – coarse sandstone, often used for millstones
Bridleway – a path for use by walkers, cyclists and horse riders	**Quoin** – corner stone
	Sett – rectangular paving stone with curved top
Clough – a ravine or narrow valley	**Tor** – a bare or rocky peak
Drystone wall – a stone wall built without using mortar	**Waymark** – a signpost marking out a route

Gritstone landscape, Peak District,

Peak District overview map

derby group

above: **Hamps Valley, north of Ilam** below: **Belper's East and North Mills**

The Chevin and the Derwent Valley Heritage Way from Belper

WALK INFORMATION

Start/Finish: Belper town centre, railway station

Access: The transpeak Manchester to Nottingham bus (service hourly), also R6.1 from Derby. National rail from Derby and Nottingham

Distance: 6½ miles (10.5 km). OS Map: Explorer 259

The walk: A circular route starting and ending at Belper, easily accessible on public transport

The pubs: King William, Milford; Holly Bush Inn, Makeney; Wheel Inn, Dead Poet's Inn, both Holbrook; Cross Keys, Belper

Belper started industrial life producing nails, but was transformed by the philanthropic Strutt family who, along with Richard Arkwright at Cromford, introduced the factory system to the textile industry. Today it's a town of two halves — the handsome and well-built workers' houses and the mills co-existing with some dismal modern estates straight from the catalogue books of the national volume builders. The walk is full of industrial and social history as well as some fine scenery, particularly over the ridge of the Chevin. There are a couple of steep sections but overall it's a fairly easy walk that is well-signed despite being outside the National Park. A great choice of attractive pubs with perhaps the widest beer choice of any of the walks makes this one a walk you'll want to return to.

Start at Belper's railway station and take the alleyway by the supermarket and the Railway pub to King Street, the main shopping street, where you turn left and after a short dis-

tance first left again into Green Lane. This leads you into the older part of town. Look out for some of Strutt's famous cluster houses (blocks of four houses, semi-detached and back-to-back, each

Houses originally built by Strutt for his workers

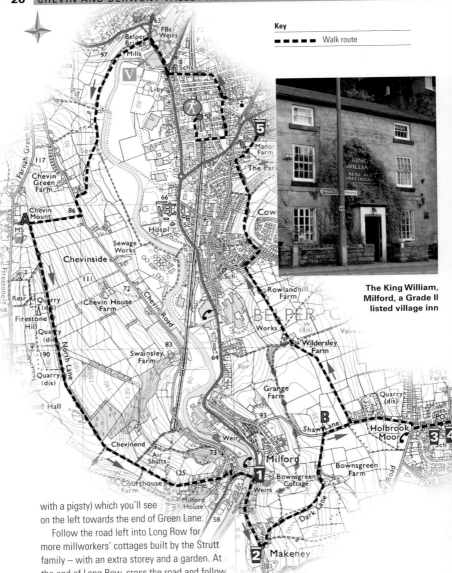

Key

■ ■ ■ ■ ■ Walk route

The King William,
Milford, a Grade II
listed village inn

with a pigsty) which you'll see
on the left towards the end of Green Lane.

Follow the road left into Long Row for
more millworkers' cottages built by the Strutt
family – with an extra storey and a garden. At
the end of Long Row, cross the road and follow
the left fork into Bridge Foot with the imposing
East Mill (1912) on your right dwarfing Strutt's
earlier North Mill (1804) which houses a Heritage
Centre with limited opening hours. (An excellent
heritage trail pamphlet guiding you round old
Belper is available from the Derwent Valley Mills
Heritage website: www.derwentvalleymills.org).
Admire the sizeable weir and millpond to the

right as you cross the Derwent before
taking the footpath immediately left over the
bridge into meadows with the Chevin (with
mast atop) ahead.

The town is soon left behind, although sadly
not the droning of traffic on the A6. At a stile
and cottages reached after a short while, ignore
the right forking path and keep straight ahead

Chevin trackway, possibly predating the Roman occupation

on the meadows with the river close by, but a couple of minutes later peel off right, through another stile, on a narrow path gently uphill into the trees. With some well-laid setts (stone blocks set into the road like cobbles) higher up, this looks like an old packhorse route – probably from the ancient Portway (see below) into Belper. The path finally joins Chevin Road by some houses. Turn left here and in 100 yards a signed footpath heads right and straight uphill to join, and turn left onto a wide bridleway (North Lane) on the Chevin (A, 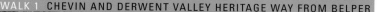 337469). This fine track is part of the Portway (see also Walk 11) which may have been a Roman track linking the fort of Little Chester at Derby with Buxton, but also possibly pre-dating the Roman occupation. Walk on, climbing over the Chevin until you start to descend, here there are good views opening out southwards towards Derby. Beyond the golf course the bridleway bears left and leads you down into the old industrial settlement of Milford, where at one time the Strutts established several further mills. A large one still remains on the river bank, although no longer producing textiles. It's right in front of you as you reach the main A6 road. Follow past the mill across the river to your first pub, the **King William 1**.

This free house, part of a handsome terrace, has had various recent ups and downs, but currently four handpumps dispense draught Bass or Marston's Pedigree, Taylor Landlord and changing guest beers. The interior has been opened out and has moved tentatively but not tackily upmarket. The pub also offers accommodation with three pleasant ensuite twin rooms. The next

stop is very close: looking back at the bridge you've just crossed, turn left down Makeney Lane for about 350 yards, fork left again into Holly Bush Lane and up to the **Holly Bush Inn 2**.

This *Good Beer Guide* regular oozes character, its multi-roomed interior includes a gem of a snug, separated from the corridor by a wood and glass partition and housing an old-fashioned range. The well-travelled Dick Turpin, having terrorised much of the south of England, apparently managed to find time to stop off at this pub too. No children are allowed inside but there is an equally characterful conservatory for them at the rear. The array of handpumps dispense a varying range of interesting beers.

Leaving the Holly Bush Inn turn left but rather than retracing your steps down the hill take the little path – Dark Lane – on the corner which quickly becomes an atmospheric sunken trackway (ignore the footpath over the stile left into the field). Follow this old route, with occasional views left over the Chevin, until it joins a tarred lane (Shaw Lane, B, 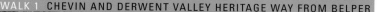 355454). Turn right and

The characterful snug at the Holly Bush Inn

walk up this minor road to the T-junction. The Miners' Welfare building just before the junction is a relic of the days of the Derbyshire coalfields. Holbrook grew to house mining families, although the pit was a couple of miles further east at Denby. It's almost straight across into Chapel Street and downhill to the first of two pubs in this lane, the **Wheel Inn** 3 .

The enthusiastic management at the Wheel have made this pub a real ale destination, with three beer festivals a year, and five handpumps offering Black Sheep Bitter and Caledonian Deuchars IPA, as well as a changing and democratically elected (by the locals) guest beer! Dogs are welcome, as are children until 9.30pm. An excellent rear conservatory overlooks a pleasant garden. It's a place you might wish to linger especially if you're staying locally and thanks to the next pub a few yards away, Chapel Street is akin to a permanent beer festival.

The interior of the **Dead Poet's Inn** 4 is so authentic that you feel you're in an untouched ancient building. In fact, it's quite a modern conversion but very well done and complemented by an excellent range of changing cask ales served from five handpumps, thanks to what looks like an enlightened policy by owners Everards.

A cautionary sign at the Dead Poet's Inn

Retrace your steps to the Miners' Welfare building and back down Shaw Lane, almost to where you joined the it, but pick up a footpath on the right just beyond the houses. This pleasant path with fine views ahead skirts Wildersley Farm (ignore the path off to the left and keep straight ahead on the farm track) bringing you out into the southern suburbs of Belper. Turn right and walk up the street to the top of the hill where you take a footpath sharp left (not straight ahead) and from here follow the purple and yellow Derwent Valley Heritage Way (DVHW) signs straight into Belper.

After an unpromising start this turns into another excellent short path through park and woodland. You emerge (with luck) into a car park and exit this slightly to the left to come out right by the **Cross Keys** 5 . Enjoying something of a renaissance since being acquired by Bateman's, this pub offers a wide range of their own fine ales here (unlike at the Dead Poet's Inn), alongside a range of snacks. This friendly and quiet two-bar local still has bar billiards, which your author spent many hours trying to master as a student…

Here, you're very close to the starting point and public transport, 5 minutes' walk away. Best ask for directions in the Cross Keys if unsure.

PUB INFORMATION

1 King William
The Bridge, Milford
Belper, Derbyshire DE56 0RR
01332 840842
Hours: 5.30 (12 Sat)-11.30;
12.30-11 Sun
Food: lunchtime snacks
Well-behaved children welcome

2 Holly Bush Inn
Holly Bush Lane, Makeney
Belper, Derbyshire DE56 0RX
01332 841729
Hours: 12-3, 5-11; 12-11 Fri & Sat;
12-10.30 Sun
Food: lunchtimes and evenings
Children in conservatory only
CAMRA Regional Inventory

3 Wheel Inn
Chapel Street, Holbrook
Derbyshire DE56 0TQ
01332 880006

www.thewheelinnholbrook.co.uk
Hours: 12-3, 5-midnight; 12-1.30am
Fri & Sat; 12-11 Sun
Food: lunchtimes and evenings
Children welcome until 9.30pm

4 Dead Poet's Inn
Chapel Street, Holbrook
Derbyshire DE56 0TQ
01332 780301
Hours: 12-2.30, 5-11; 12-11 Fri &
Sat; 12-10.30 Sun
Food: lunchtime meals and snacks
Children in conservatory only
(until 8pm)

5 Cross Keys
35 Market Place, Belper
Derbyshire DE56 1FZ
01773 599191
Hours: 12-11 (10.30 Sun)
Food: snacks only

TRY ALSO:

Queen's Head
29 Chesterfield Rd, Belper
Derbyshire DE56 1FF
01773 825525
www.derbyshirepubs.co.uk
Hours: 4 (12 Fri & Sat)-11; 12-10.30
Sun

Local attractions: Strutt's North
Mill and Belper Heritage Walk;
Crich Tramway Museum, 2 miles;
Arkwright's Cromford Mill, 5 miles;
Kedleston Hall (National Trust), 5
miles; Darley Abbey Mills (part of
World Heritage Site), 5 miles.

Carsington Water via the Back Door

WALK INFORMATION

Start/Finish: Hulland Ward, Black Horse Inn (261470)

Access: Service 109 (Arriva) from Derby; bus 113 from Belper & Ashbourne

Distance: 6½ miles (10.5 km). OS Maps: Explorer 259, OL24

The walk: A more challenging circular route, outside the National Park, with limited access by public transport

The pubs: Barley Mow Inn, Kirk Ireton; Black Horse Inn, Hulland Ward. Option to visit Red Lion Inn, Hognaston

The landscape between Derby and the southern fringe of the National Park is rural and green and the route here is undulating but nowhere dauntingly steep. However, be aware that navigation on this walk can be a little tricky because many of the paths are infrequently used, as is common outside the National Park, and some of the stiles are well hidden. But don't let this put you off this excellent country saunter — the pubs really are in the top league. Public transport is limited, especially in the evening: if you're out for the day without a car, you might want to consider a taxi back to Belper or Ashbourne, both a few miles away. The walk is designed to reach the Barley Mow at lunchtime, and allow plenty of time for a leisurely afternoon before the Black Horse opens at 6pm.

The walk starts at the Black Horse Inn in Hulland Ward (261470) which, all being well, you'll be able to visit at the end of the walk. If you've arrived by car it's OK to leave it in the car park on the understanding that you will be patronising the pub in due course! Start by taking the minor road (Moss Lane) running northwest away from the A517 at the far end of the car park; take the footpath to the right after about 450 yards and follow the hedge for a couple of fields before

The open expanses of Carsington Water, an important haven for waterfowl

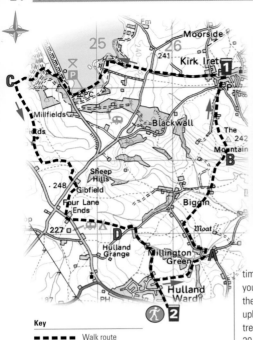

The Barley Mow Inn, one of Derbyshire's most unspoilt pubs

Key

■ ■ ■ ■ Walk route

veering left into a wooded area and dropping to a stile and into a clough fed by two tiny streams, a charmingly hidden spot. Follow the path around a fallen tree through some holly and over a rickety stile to a small lane (A, ◉ 264477). Turn left here steeply uphill, disregarding the first footpath sign and continuing past some cottages and Milners Farm on your left. The next building on the right is Meadows Farm. There is no sign but turn right here through the yard between the house and the barn, go through a rusty iron gate and then another, and head straight downhill switching to the adjacent field on your right to keep the hedge immediately on your left. Hay Farm will appear ahead of you – head through the lowest field (it may be overgrown) to find a stile and plank bridge in the far left-hand corner of the field. Cross this and emerge on a farm track with the farm itself on your immediate right. Congratulate yourself on your safe arrival amid probable fanfares of bird song, before looking for the next hidden stile in the hedge about 30 yards left of the farm. Once over this, strike straight uphill through three fields getting steeper all the

time. You'll be rewarded with great views behind you. At the top of the third field (B, ◉ 265490) the line of the path bears a little to the left, still uphill, towards and along a hedge with mature trees. You'll find another stile on the right some 30 yards before the end of the field. Pass through here and up to another stile after 50 yards, across the next field, which takes you onto a shady track. Once on this track, climb almost immediately over another stile and bear left into the wired paddocks – gates take you through these and lead you up to a further gate onto a wide track from where it's plain sailing right into Kirk Ireton. A secluded village perched high above the Ecclesbourne Valley, it became a dairy farming community although the large farmhouses that used to line the village street have gone.

After the foregoing there is no way that you can miss the **Barley Mow Inn 1**, just a few yards from the small village green. Nowhere else in this book will a pint have been so well earned as the one drunk here! This wonderful Jacobean building deserves the many superlatives that have been bestowed upon it. In the simple multi-roomed interior (note the recycled billiard table slates in the main bar), service is dispensed from a small hatch behind which an excellent variety of beers is stillaged. Expect about five cask ales usually from small independent micro-breweries, with Whim Hartington IPA a regular. Like everything else here food is staunchly traditional:

a range of good-value lunchtime rolls. Children can be brought into the pub at lunchtimes only and then not into the main bar. At the time of writing, the shop and post office set up in an outbuilding of the pub remain a valuable village service. The good quality accommodation above is owned and run by the pub, if you want to stay for B&B here.

The Barley Mow shuts at 2pm and the Black Horse opens at 6pm. This gives you plenty of time to enjoy the excellent scenery on the way back and also time to make the odd mistake finding your way back to Hulland Ward! Leaving the same way you came in, pick up a footpath with a weathered wooden sign to Hognaston a few yards on the right down Blackwall Lane. This leads you across the meadows in a pretty straight line to reach the reservoir in about 20 to 25 minutes (veer slightly right by the stone trough and spring). Join the 'Long Trail' – a cycle route and path that circumnavigates the reservoir. Bear left, keeping close to the water's edge, to arrive at Millfields (with toilets etc) in a few minutes. The grassy slopes at the water's edge might also make a good spot for a summer siesta. Continue on the main track for a few more minutes and just before the memorial to the four young men killed in 1984 (when the embankment of the reservoir collapsed whilst under construction) the track veers left; follow this and cross over a stile and the fast road with care. Go down a waymarked tarred track with extensive views that curves downhill until it meets another

CARSINGTON WATER

Carsington Water is one of the Peak's newest reservoirs, and the ninth largest in England. Work began in 1979, after much planning, but in 1984 part of the original dam collapsed, at which point it was levelled to its foundations. In 1989 work on the new design began and in 1992 it was finally opened by HM the Queen and became an instant tourist attraction.

Careful landscaping including the planting of some half a million trees and shrubs has reduced the impact of the reservoir on the environment. In 1995, Severn Trent Water received a 'Forestry Centre of Excellence' award for using 'the highest standards of woodland management'. It is now an important destination for water birds.

The reservoir is owned and operated by Severn Trent Water and is part of a water compensation scheme. This means that water is pumped here from the River Derwent at times of high rainfall, stored in the reservoir and returned to the Derwent when the river level would otherwise be too low to allow water extraction for treatment (and therefore drinking) further downstream. No water is actually extracted from Carsington Water itself. There is an excellent Visitor Centre (open daily from 10am with a permanent exhibition) together with a café and restaurant. The site also has wheelchair access.

good track, at which point turn left and through a couple of gates onto another path to join the road at Hognaston Bridge (C, 🔵 240499). The *Red Lion Inn* (🔵 234506) in the village is an option here, about half a mile right along the

A popular tourist attraction, Carsington Water reservoir

road, but be aware that it closes in the afternoon between 3–6pm. If you do make it, expect four beers: Marston's Pedigree and Burton Bitter, plus two local micro-brewery guest ales.

The path from here to Gibfield ( 247487) looks very straightforward on the map – it strikes off left immediately uphill but keep your wits about you as it darts through a hawthorn hedge after about 150 yards via a stile. Follow the hedge (now on your right) but be aware the next stile is about 50 yards down from the field corner. Then follow the angle of the waymarked sign to another wooden stile and keep straight ahead through a metal gate. Here on your left, at the time of writing, there was an impromptu stage with lights, but bear slightly uphill now and look for a double stile over a very small, dry valley and continue uphill, close to a hedge on your right. A large house should appear ahead. Look out for a sizable pond (not on the map) and keep it on your left (approx 245492). Make for the dominant tree slightly left, a useful landmark which as you approach has a wooden framework around the lower trunk. Turn 90 degrees left here at the tree and follow the hedge keeping it on your left through a couple of stiles and then bear half right on an apology for a path uphill to the lane at Gibfield. Phew!

Now across the road the footpath sign points outside of and around the fence and gate to a hidden stile into a field. Go across here and over one new stile and through one new gate before turning right in the shallow valley up to and through a metal gate (no sign), which leads

The plain interior of the Barley Mow Inn, in keeping with the building's Jacobean origins

you across to a farmyard. Walk through the tractors and sludge gulpers to the road. Turn left (no pavement, take care) for about 75 paces and locate a hidden stile through a holly and hawthorn hedge into a field. Now make for the large oak across the field bearing slightly right and go through the metal gate a few yards to the right of it. Head for the telegraph pole and then another up ahead, by a few prominent trees, and you should see the buildings of the Grange (D, 254481) ahead of you. Now, about 25 yards to the right of the telegraph pole, the most overgrown stile in Derbyshire takes you through a hedge of hawthorn and holly, then it's easy to follow the hedge down towards the Grange. The path actually veers right immediately before them to join the lane at a stile and sign.

From here the rest is relatively simple: take the right fork just beyond the buildings and follow this lane (Moss Lane) all the way back to the car park of the **Black Horse Inn 2**. At this point you can award yourself an orienteering gold star before sampling the fine ales in the pub, which offers an interesting beer and food menu. The current management have enthusiastically turned the Black Horse from an also ran into a *Good Beer Guide* fixture – you can certainly expect a warm welcome in this modernised but still characterful pub.

PUB INFORMATION

1 Barley Mow Inn
Main Street, Kirk Ireton
Ashbourne, Derbyshire DE6 3JP
01335 370306
Hours: 12–2, 7–11 (10.30 Sun)
Food: lunchtime snacks
CAMRA National Inventory

2 Black Horse Inn
Hulland Ward, Ashbourne
Derbyshire DE6 3EE
01335 370206
Hours: 12–2.30, 6–11; 12–3,
7–10.30 Sun
Food: 12–2, 6–9.30; 12–2,
7–9.30 Sun

TRY ALSO:

Red Lion Inn
Hognaston, Ashbourne
Derbyshire DE6 1PR
01335 370396

Local attractions: Carsington Water
Visitor Centre; Wirksworth – historic
market town with a Heritage Centre,
5 miles; Ashbourne – historic market
town, 4 miles; Belper North Mill,
6 miles.

The Manifold Valley and Wetton, from Ilam

WALK INFORMATION

Start/Finish: Ilam Hall car park

Access: Public transport is very limited. Buses from Ashbourne on Thursdays and Saturdays only

Distance: 8 miles (13 km). OS Map: Explorer OL24

The walk: The walking is not too strenuous although there are a couple of steep hills; route finding is generally straightforward except just before Castern Hall

The pubs: Royal Oak, Wetton; Watts Russell Arms, Hopedale

The Hamps at Rushley Bridge, near Ilam

A circular walk in quintessential limestone country, with steep valleys and rounded hills covered in short grass divided by grey walls. There is plenty of interest, and you will have earned a pint by the time you get to the pub! This is probably a walk to save for a pleasant day, for the tops can be quite exposed in a cool wind or squall. The start point, Ilam (see information box) is better known as the gateway to Dovedale, one of the prettiest (and busiest) of the Dales; this walk however is guaranteed to get you away from the crowds!

Start at the car park at the rear of the Youth Hostel, Ilam Hall (131507) and from there make your way down to the pretty River Hamps which flows around the grounds to the east in a majestic sweeping curve. The idyllic start to the walk is maintained as you traverse a narrow section of the limestone valley before it opens out. After a few minutes cross the river on the footbridge and take the path forking right over the brow leading directly to the road by the farm at Rushley, with lovely expansive views across the peaceful valley.

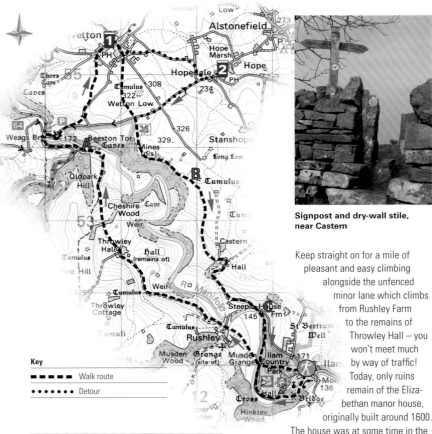

Signpost and dry-wall stile, near Castern

Key

■ ■ ■ ■ Walk route

● ● ● ● ● ● Detour

Keep straight on for a mile of pleasant and easy climbing alongside the unfenced minor lane which climbs from Rushley Farm to the remains of Throwley Hall – you won't meet much by way of traffic! Today, only ruins remain of the Elizabethan manor house, originally built around 1600. The house was at some time in the hands of Charles Cotton, Isaac Walton's fishing companion, but is now in the hands of English Heritage. Go through the farmyard, (the modern hall is a beef farm), following the rather indistinct route uphill northwestwards, keeping a wall on your right, until you come to the brow of the hill. Ahead of you lies a wonderful view and you can trace the route of what is to come – walk down to the dry valley below and then on to the river at Beeston Tor Farm (A, ◉ 105540).

Importantly, although the map seems to suggest otherwise, there is no crossing of the River Hamps at this point – that said the river is dry at some times of the year (the limestone river bed is sufficiently permeable to allow the river to dive underground occasionally). You'll probably need to follow the river upstream past the farm and across the Manifold following the

ILAM

Ilam occupies an enviably agreeable position on the banks of the River Hamps close to its confluence with the Dove. Sometime in the 11th century a small monastic settlement was established by the monks of Burton-on-Trent Abbey and, after the dissolution of the monasteries, this was purchased by the Port family who owned the estate for the next 300 years and established the first Ilam Hall. In 1820 the Ilam estate was bought by Jesse Watts-Russell, a wealthy industrialist who moved the village away from the hall and the now rather isolated church and rebuilt it in the distinctive pseudo-alpine style we see today. The centre of the village is dominated by a memorial cross, similar to Charing Cross, erected by Jesse Watts-Russell in 1840 to commemorate his wife, Mary. Its perfect proportions and graceful carved decoration have earned it great affection and admiration as well as the distinction of a Grade II* listing. The main part of Ilam Hall was demolished in the 1930s, but the remaining section is a Youth Hostel and the whole estate now belongs to the National Trust.

stream up as far as Weag's Bridge (100542) before crossing the bridge and walking steeply up the quiet Larkstone Lane above the two hairpin bends. (There is also, before climbing, the possibility of linking to the Onecote circuit – Walk 25.) When the lane straightens and the gradient eases, look for the signed route left taking you across a field (steep climb) to join Carr Lane. Carry on uphill on the lane for a minute or two before a path leaves left and crosses a field pleasantly into Wetton village – the correct path is indeed the obvious one diverging northeast from the road. Follow the houses down the lane and the **Royal Oak 1** is close to the church as the lane turns right beyond it.

The Royal Oak retains some character despite upgrading. It offers three real ales, usually Greene King Abbot and Theakston Bitter, plus a changing guest beer. Food is available and the pub offers self-catering accommodation. Its main claim to fame is as the centre of the annual world toe wrestling championships (I kid you not), held every June.

Leaving the pub turn right up the lane to the road junction. At the junction of Carr Lane and Ashburton Lane there is a path heading off between the two, ahead and right. (Here, if you need a little more refreshment, it is possible to detour to another pub. Follow the instructions in the box for the **Watts Russell Arms 2**, you will rejoin the route a little further on.) Follow the clear path through several fields taking the left option by a field barn to join and cross the road by a stile. The path is signed 'Highfields Mine & Castern' at this point. (If there is no stile opposite you've taken the wrong fork – turn left

The pretty stone-built village of Wetton

TO THE WATTS RUSSELL ARMS

At the road junction of Carr Lane and Ashburton Lane after the Royal Oak, the easiest route to the Watts Russell Arms is to take the lane left, and ignore the next two left turns. Turn right at the T-junction, left at the next (Wall Ditch), and down to the valley bottom where the pub sits. Map readers will spot a couple of small short cuts on paths. It's about a mile, but as experience has suggested some erratic opening times, it's best to ring ahead. Details of the pub are given in the Alstonefield circuit (Walk 23). Return to the route by taking the same lane but straight ahead this time, until you reach the footpath crossing at 112544 .

The Watts Russell Arms

and walk up the lane for 200 yards!) The route now takes you on a clear track along the edge of a steep slope with sublime views of the Hamps valley below, where for the geographers among you there are some very impressive ingrown meanders (where the water has cut away an overhang on one side of the riverbank). The graceful spire across the valley is Grindon church.

The rolling hills and grasslands of the Hamps Valley, north of Ilam

Eventually you'll pass through a small gate into the Castern Wood Nature Reserve – a good spot for a siesta before you make for the stile and finger post 30 yards ahead (B, 117536). Take the path signed 'Castern' by some old lead workings near Highfields Mine onto another stile and post in 75 yards. The waymarking is poor here: cross the large field at about 45 degrees away from the wall down to the opposite corner, where a gate and stile are joined by a small standing stone just beyond. Now look ahead and below you for another gate (with a large tree beyond it) and make for that. Now, once through this stile you should be able to pick out, make for and follow a good track along the wall towards Castern Hall. (Don't worry if you stray too far left as you'll pick up other tracks heading to Castern

Hall too.) Like Throwley Hall earlier, which you should still be able to see across the valley, Castern Hall was once the kernel of an agricultural hamlet. Today the house is still occupied and is pretty imposing.

Follow the path in a loop around the farm buildings and to the right alongside the tarred lane which leads you down to the valley floor at River Lodge (C, 128517). At the Lodge a permitted path takes you to the right through a metal gate and along the riverside on an attractive trail. When you reach the point where you crossed the bridge near the start of the walk, you can either head left up the path which climbs over to the village in less than half a mile; or retrace your steps along the river back to Ilam Hall and the car park.

The beautiful scenery of the Manifold Valley, an important wildlife habitat

PUB INFORMATION

1 Royal Oak
Wetton, Nr Ashbourne
Derbyshire DE6 2AG
01335 310287
Hours: Closed Mon; 12–2.30
(not Tue), 7 (8 Tue)–11; 12–3,
7–10.30 Sat–Sun
Food: lunchtimes and
evenings (not Tue)
Children in lounge only

2 Watts Russell Arms
Hope Dale, Alstonefield
Staffordshire DE6 2GD

01335 310126
www.wattsrussell.co.uk
Hours: Closed Mon (except bank
hol); 12–2, 6.30–10 Tue-Thu;
12–10.30 Fri; 12–11 Sat; 12–9 Sun
Food: 12–2 (4 Sat), 7–9; 12–4,
6–8 Sun

Local attractions: Dovedale,
approximately ½ mile; Ashbourne
(market town), 3 miles; Ilam Park and
National Trust tea rooms at Ilam Hall,
adjacent; Tissington Trail, 2 miles.

matlock bath group

Arkwright's Cromford Mill

Matlock to Cromford via Lumsdale and Bonsall

WALK INFORMATION

Start: Matlock Rail or bus station

Finish: Matlock Bath (shorter walk) or Bell Inn, Cromford

Access: Rail services from Matlock and Matlock Bath; local buses 17, 64 to start of walk, see *Peak District Bus Timetable*

Distance: 3¼ miles (5 km) to Matlock Bath; 4½ miles to Bonsall; 6 miles (9½ km) to Cromford (add ⅔ mile/1 km to Barley Mow Inn and back). OS Map: Explorer OL24

The walk: A longer route that can be split into two if necessary

The pubs: White Lion Inn, Starkholmes; County & Station Hotel, Princess Victoria, Temple Hotel, all Matlock Bath; King's Head, Barley Mow Inn, both Bonsall; Boat Inn, Bell Inn, both Cromford

This is a rewarding and flexible route, suitable for a half-day trip if you finish at Matlock Bath, and quite possible as a day trip starting from Derby or Nottingham and taking the train to Matlock. You could also split the route into two walks, breaking at Matlock Bath. Industrial archaeology and good views abound in a rewarding transect through one of the geographical highlights of the Peak. It's mainly downhill if you take the bus to Bentley Bridge, but otherwise just one long steep climb out of Matlock Bath. Plenty of good pubs to choose from.

👤 Start from Matlock station (it has a convenient and large car park). If you're a purist or possibly a masochist, get to the start proper by walking about a mile steeply uphill across the river (straight up Bank Road from the roundabout, over Smedley Road and right at the top to merge into the A632 by the Duke of Wellington). Carry on north as far as Bentley Bridge where Lumsdale Road runs off right. Lesser mortals are strongly

Nearing the top of the climb out of Bonsall on to the Barley Mow Inn

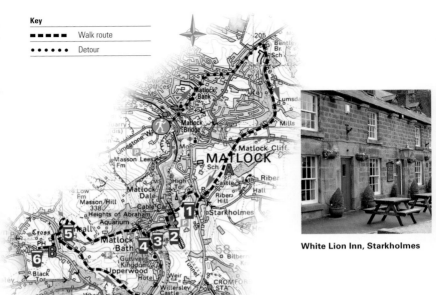

White Lion Inn, Starkholmes

advised to take the Chesterfield local bus, route 17, which runs hourly from the bus station, or a taxi. Ask for Lumsdale Road, which is the stop for Highfields School.

Once on Lumsdale Road the transition from suburban street to countryside is rapid. Carry on along the rough lane (footpath sign) 200 yards past the school to a pleasant millpond by some attractive cottages. Here, we're at the top of a remarkable cascade as the brook drops precipitously through Lumsdale in one of the hidden gems of Derbyshire's rich industrial past (see information box). Thanks to the vision and tenacity of Marjorie Mills, a local landowner, and later the Arkwright Society who currently lease the land, the overgrown remains of several atmospheric old mills which occupied the valley here have been left to decay gracefully in a charming sylvan setting. Follow the path carefully down the surprisingly steep valley and it will eventually rejoin the quiet lane, which runs down the valley between odd collections of old industrial buildings, some of which are still in use.

Simply follow this lane left down to the main road (A615), unfortunately the best scenic goodies are behind us on this stretch at least. Turn right and after 50 yards, opposite a path (signed), you go on a gentle climb across the hillside above Matlock (ignore footpath sign leading uphill left), up wooden steps and over a slippery walk-board with excellent views to the right over the town below you (A, ⊙ 305594). Above you lies the late Victorian folly of Riber Castle, which dominates Matlock. Built by local industrialist John Smedley, Riber Castle is where he lived briefly but the castellated outline, which looks imposing from afar, is rather disappointing close up – you can walk steeply up from the scissor path junction and visit, returning the same way.

If, however, the first pint of the day beckons, continue ahead to some houses, the outposts of the lofty village of Starkholmes, before reaching the Riber Road on a sharp bend. Drop downhill to join the Starkholmes Road below another hairpin bend, and turn left to reach the **White Lion Inn 1** after about 100 yards. This is a long, open-plan building which caters for diners and retains its flagged floor in the bar area. The pub offers Marston's Pedigree along with up to four changing guest ales, many from the Marston's portfolio along with freshly cooked food (except

LUMSDALE AND THE MILLS OF BENTLEY BROOK

A remarkable number of industries have utilised this valley since the first record of a mill here in the 17th century. Taking their cue from the revolutionary developments of Richard Arkwright down in nearby Cromford, the industries include lead smelting, textile bleaching, haberdashery, lambswool spinning, a sawmill, paint mill, hosiery manufacturers and a very successful tape and shawl factory.

Shawl and tape makers Lowe & Scholes' great mills were powered by water from five dams and two massive water-wheels, each one over 40 ft in diameter. The last textiles firm in the valley, operated until the late 1990s.

As the buildings in the upper section of the valley fell out of use, they were abandoned and allowed to become derelict. The valley, which once had been known for the stark beauty of its rocky outcrops, well-manicured ponds and its waterfall became thickly wooded, dark and forgotten. In 1939 the land alongside the mills was purchased by Marjorie Mills, who fell in love with the area. Despite many offers for the stone, she refused to

allow demolition of the mill structures and the area became a welcome haven for wildlife and a future treasure for a later generation's awakening interest in industrial archaeology. In later life she leased the site to the Arkwright Society for a peppercorn rent on the condition that it was nurtured and opened for the public.

Atmospheric mill ruin, Lumsdale

Monday). It's also family friendly – there's a separate children's menu.

On leaving the White Lion Inn, return to the Riber Road junction then continue north for another 150 yards where a footpath (to Matlock Bath) points left down High Tor Road. This soon gives way to an open descent into Derbyshire's inland spa resort, which on a summer weekend resembles Brighton minus the beach. As you reach the foot of this path a range of sights greets you – the entrance to the High Tor grounds and the Heights of Abraham cable car – before

the path dives under the railway and over the river. This brings you to your next refreshment stop. the **County & Station Hotel** 2. This is on the first corner as you reach the parade and is a reliable real ale outlet which sometimes hosts beer festivals. Beers are from the Marstons range which includes the Jennings and Banks's portfolios. Further south along South Parade, near the tourist information centre, is another agreeable pub, the **Princess Victoria** 3 named after the visit of the would-be queen to the town in 1832. This is a Bateman's house, so expect their Dark Mild, XB, XXXB, alongside Greene King Abbot and other guest beers. Food is available all day every day. In addition, if you are seduced by the range of beers and the climb up to Bonsall is beginning to look daunting, you could go the whole hog and spoil yourself at the excellent **Temple**

Temple Hotel, a staunch supporter of local independent breweries

Hotel **4**. It's up the steep Temple Road then take a right turn beyond the pavillion – signed to Gulliver's Kingdom. This free house with a courtyard welcomes all and is a firm supporter of local independent breweries: the three handpumps dispense mainly Derbyshire beers such as Thornbridge, Whim and Leatherbritches. The hotel also holds mini beer festivals. If Matlock Bath is as far as you're going, then the promenade – North and South Parade – offers a range of earthly delights from

The friendly Barley Mow Inn, often with live music in the evening

chip shops, amusements and other fleshpots as well as a pleasant riverside walk.

There are plenty of buses back to Matlock or trains to Derby if you've had enough now. There's also an excellent high level walk over the picturesque limestone crag of High Tor into Matlock. To do this, return to the point where the footpath brought you into Matlock Bath and close to the cable car entrance, a path directs you over High Tor towards Matlock. In all events consult your map or ask in the tourist office.

Returning to the main route, back in Matlock Bath, a short distance north, back up the parade from the Princess Victoria is Waterloo Road. Walk up here and after 50 yards take a cobbled footpath steeply uphill to the left. Cross a road and continue uphill into West Bank. As you ascend great views open up behind you across to Riber castle. This path brings you out at West Lodge by the cable car exit. Pausing to draw breath, bear left onto the lane, with more uphill work to do. Another 200 yards further, by a large house and just before a double garage, a path leads discreetly right into the trees. There's no respite up through the wooded hillside, and you may be regretting that last pint (or two) down below! Ignore paths joining from the right, until eventually you reach the summit by a stile, where splendid views open up southwards towards the Black Rocks, easily identifiable by the TV mast at Bolehill, and the hilltop village of

Middleton by Wirksworth (where the writer D. H. Lawrence lived for one year).

Pass through the stile and turn right joining a track passing Ember farm on your right. The village immediately below you is Cromford. Walk a short way along here and turn right by a field barn onto a marked footpath and follow this across the fields with grand views across the wooded valley, the Via Gellia, below you. The Latin name comes from the Gell family of Wirksworth who had the route built. You should be able to pick out Bonsall church spire immediately below you as you walk, but the village itself lies tucked away in a fold of the landscape. Ignore the first set of branch paths at the stile and continue downhill to a muddy corner of a field where, through a gate and stile just beyond, you join a wider track (B, ◉ 281586). This well-made route was a former path to fluorspar mines on the hillside above Bonsall. Go down the steep hill, taking care in wet or icy conditions, to emerge in the charming village centre where, by the phone box, there is an excellent mounted pictogram packed with interesting information about Bonsall's history.

Dominating the quiet and tiny market place with its stone cross is the imposing **King's Head 5**. In terms of vernacular architecture this is one of the finest pub exteriors in the county, with its dressed sandstone quoins (the large corner stones that strengthen the walls) setting off the well proportioned three-storey building. This is another Bateman's house serving a full range of snacks and meals. It is also pretty family-friendly, and has a cosy and dark atmospheric interior. The village is fortunate to retain two good pubs. To get to the second, take a path out of the village where, opposite the far gable of the King's Head, there is a Limestone Way sign on a post. Head for the steps before following the walled path uphill. It's fairly steep at first but gets easier. As you go through a stile before some old lead spoil heaps, take the left forking path through a second squeezer stile to pick up a good grass path leading left downhill into the dale and the **Barley Mow Inn** 6.

In a peaceful setting, this free house may not have the architectural gravitas of the King's Head but it compensates with a friendly welcome and great beer, with Whim Hartington a regular and a changing guest beer. Alan, the friendly landlord who has clocked up almost 20 years

here, is renowned for his guided walks and hosting a range of events including lively music sessions. Food is available and children allowed until 8.30pm but do note that the pub is closed weekday lunchtimes.

Return to the main village square (walk up the tarmac drive situated immediately downhill from the pub and look for the five-bar gate beyond and to the left of the house, then cross the fields to the stile and carry on down the hill). Take Church Street, which runs up to the right beyond the King's Head, past the primary school and church before it peters out into a path by Townend farm. Follow this path gently uphill along a wall, picking up and following a fence around an old quarry (⊙ 287574). As you go along more views are revealed south to Black Rocks (look for the mast) and the large working quarry below, a reminder of the continuing uneasy relationship between extractive industry and tourism in the Peak. The path turns downhill and narrows through

Stone squeezer stile and signed footpath near Bonsall

hawthorn saplings to join a wider, curving downhill track. Another 150 yards further on, follow the fence when it turns sharp right into trees on a good track. Select the downhill route, picking up a rickety metal fence on your right – you'll hear traffic sounds from the Via Gellia far below through the trees. This route takes you pleasantly down towards Cromford. Just before the houses, fork left (slightly uphill) to traverse above the terraced gardens, ignoring the next left fork and emerging via a narrow cobbled exit into the village close to Cromford's mill pond. The route is easier to follow than it sounds!

The Scarthin bookshop, by the pond, is something of a local institution, with a labyrinthine interior that hides a lively 'What's On' board and a charming little café upstairs – it is truly not to be missed! A little further on is the **Boat Inn** **7**. This is a cosy pub, retaining much character despite the alterations, and offers good food along with a tempting range of locally sourced

beers. For a different atmosphere in this early industrial village, pass Richard Arkwright's Greyhound Inn in the market square just beyond the pond (noting the chip shop perhaps, for later usage) and head right to the **Bell Inn** **8**, 150 yards further up the hill (at time of writing only open in the evenings during the week). Another listed building guarding the stunningly intact North Street terraces, this former Kimberley house serves Hardys & Hansons and other Greene King beers in a nicely traditional multi-roomed building. There's no kitchen here so you'll need to go elsewhere to eat.

There are more good pubs to consider in Matlock. The *Boat House*, close to the footpath from Matlock Bath on the main road between the two, is a former Kimberley house and a *Good Beer Guide* regular, with a nice pubby atmosphere. The *Thorn Tree*, on Jackson Road up on the hillside close to the Council offices, is a steep climb but for beer devotees well worth it!

PUB INFORMATION

1 White Lion Inn
195 Starkholmes Road, Starkholmes
Matlock, Derbyshire DE4 5JA
01629 582511
www.whitelionmatlock.co.uk
Hours: 12-2 (not Mon-Tue), 5-11
(11.30 Wed, midnight Fri); 12-midnight Sat; 12-11 Sun
Food: 12-2 (not Tue), 5.30-9;
12-3 Sun

2 County & Station Hotel
258-260 Dale Road
Matlock Bath, Derbyshire DE4 3NT
01629 580802
www.countyandstation.co.uk
Hours: 12-midnight (1am Fri & Sat)
Food: lunchtimes and evenings

3 Princess Victoria
174-176 South Parade, Matlock
Bath, Derbyshire DE4 3NR
01629 57462
Hours: 12-11 (10.30 Sun)
No Children under 14
Food: all day, every day

4 Temple Hotel
Temple Walk, Matlock Bath
Derbyshire DE4 3PG.
01629 583911
www.templehotel.co.uk
Hours: 12-11 (10 Sun)
Food: 12–9 (8 Sun)
Welcomes children for meals

5 King's Head
62 Yeoman Street, Bonsall
Matlock, Derbyshire DE4 2AA.
01629 822703
Hours: 12-2.30 (not Mon-Tue), 6.30
(9 Mon)-11; 12-2.30, 6.30-10.30 Sun

6 Barley Mow Inn
The Dale, Bonsall
Matlock, Derbyshire DE4 2AY
01629 825685
www.barleymowbonsall.co.uk
Hours: closed Mon; 6-11Tue-Fri;
12-11 Sat; 12-10.30 Sun
Food: 6-9 Tue-Fri; 12–3, 6–9
Sat-Sun

7 Boat Inn
Scarthin, Cromford
Matlock, Derbyshire DE4 3QF
01629 823282
Hours: 12–3, 6 (7 Sat)–11; 12-3,
7-10.30 Sun
Food: lunchtimes and evenings

8 Bell Inn
47 Cromford Hill, Cromford
Matlock, Derbyshire DE4 3RF
01629 822102
Hours: 7-11; 12-3, 7-11 Sat; 12-3,
7-10.30 Sun
No food available

**The Bell Inn, Arkwright's
development, North
Street, Cromford**

TRY ALSO:

Boat House
110 Dale Road, Matlock,
Derbyshire DE4 3PP
01629 581519
Hours: 11.30-2.30, 5-11.30;
11.30-11.30 Wed-Sat; 11.30-10.30 Sun
Food: lunchtimes and evenings

Thorn Tree
48 Jackson Road
Matlock, Derbyshire DE4 3JQ
01629 582923
Hours: 12-2 (not Mon-Tue), 6-11;
12-2.30, 5-midnight Fri; 12-midnight
Sat; 12-11.30 Sun
Food: lunchtimes and evenings

Local attractions: Historic Cromford and Arkwright's Mill; Peak district Mining Museum, Matlock Bath; Heights of Abraham via cable car, Matlock Bath; Riber Castle folly, Matlock; Peak Rail Preservation Society, Matlock.

Ashover and the Amber Valley

Start: Ashover village, adjacent to parish church

Finish: Old Poets' Corner, Ashover

Access: Buses 17 and 64, Chesterfield services from Matlock

Distance: 5 miles (8 km); OS Map: Explorer 269

The walk: A valley circuit for more confident walkers

The pubs: Nettle Inn, Milltown; Old Poets' Corner, Ashover

Although the Ashover region is well outside the National Park, the scenery is of extremely high quality. The River Amber cuts a deep valley south of the village of Ashover and this walk covers a circuit around the valley and importantly caters for the needs of the ale connoisseur by depositing walkers back at a cracking pub festooned with CAMRA awards. Navigation needs a little care in the middle section, particularly as some signposts are missing or appear to be in different places from the map (Derbyshire County Council Officers please note) so this is certainly a walk where the liquid reward is earned.

Start in Ashover by the handsome parish church and take a path just south of the church on the right as you face downhill. You'll find yourself in the open countryside very quickly. Join a lane (Butts Road) and dropping left after 20 yards or so, take an unsigned path on the right just below the houses. Follow this up to a rusty gate and makeshift stile in

Shady path near the church in Ashover

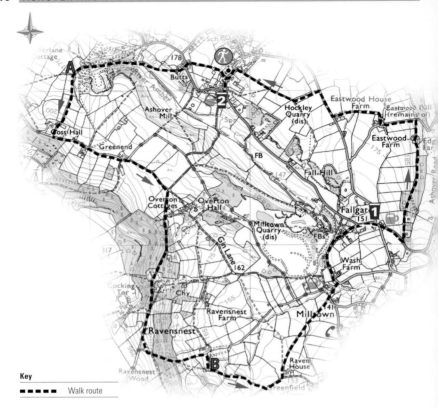

a railing beyond into a field where, bearing a little left, you drop gently downhill towards the river where a path eventually reappears to lead you through an attractive wooded stretch. Join a wider track here keeping straight ahead and just after crossing a muddy track into a disused quarry on the left, look for a stile and attractive narrow stone bridge over the stream also on your left (A, ●, 339632).

Then it's uphill through the meadows on a clear grassy track towards a telephone mast on the moor (they do have their uses after all); on your right is Goss Hall, beyond which and through a couple of squeezers you'll join a leafy lane. Turn left here and simply follow for about half a mile with pleasant rural views all around until an even larger hall comes into view (this is Overton Hall, see map). Just before reaching the hall, bear right on another unsigned bridleway that must be of some antiquity since much of

The half-timbered Old Poets' Corner, Ashover

the lower part of it is laid with substantial setts. As you head into the attractive woodland above with wide views opening out down towards the valley, the setts give way to bare earth with the path acquiring a heathland character higher up. Enjoy the views but near the top of the climb, just before the copse of trees on your left, look out for another unsigned path leading left through a stile. Once over the stile the route is clear across the meadow towards trees below you with views to Ashover village and church on the left and a reservoir to your right. Reaching the line of trees at the foot of the field and bearing right for a short while, you'll see a signed path dropping steeply through lovely woodland. Carefully make your way down here where you'll find it gets even steeper with steps lower down to the bottom. Here you should be able to make out the top of a wooden stile by a holly tree directly ahead. (Be aware that this route does not appear on the OS map for some reason.) Head for the stile and pass through. Here you'll be treated to bluebells, holly, dog rose and hawthorn before you suddenly come upon the formal garden and driveway of a large house on your right (B, 347613).

The next stretch is navigationally a bit of a mess: ignore the footpath sign leading left and instead turn right and continue about 50 yards on the driveway to pick up another marked footpath leading off slightly to the left through the fence. Now about 50 yards further look out for a new step-stile on your left in trees. Leave the good earthen path, which will lead you astray as surely as it did me, and cross this stile. Head across the meadow (there's no path) and make towards a post at the far side of the field, slightly to the right. Go through a gateless pair of posts to the left of this and then across the next field to another new wooden stile. Follow the waymarked route to the right, towards the largest trees and over a step-stile onto a green lane, where you turn left and enjoy a brief respite from the navigational difficulties.

Now, immediately before Raven House in about 150 yards, turn left off the lane and follow a path, keeping the hedge on your right until you reach a double gate. Left over the stile here on to a worn grassy path along another hedge; to keep you on your toes the path cuts through this hedge in about 75 yards but rewards you with a well-beaten track across the final field to the lane adjacent to the Miners' Arms at Milltown. Now just beyond it follow the larger lane left with initially a stream to keep you company, but then as it arcs around, head uphill to where the **Nettle Inn**  soon comes into view. The Nettle is a smart free house where an emphasis on food goes hand-in-hand with its enthusiastic real ale policy. You can enjoy a couple of beers from the local Bradfield micro-brewery plus a guest ale; you will have earned them. The Nettle also offers accommodation – phone for details.

Weathered footbridge over a stream near Ashover

The remainder of the walk is a breeze in navigational terms! Follow the lane uphill for a couple of minutes beyond the Nettle Inn taking care since there's no footpath, then double back left on a signed path with extensive views across the Amber Valley. Go boldly through the farmyard towards the end of this path and turn left downhill when you reach the lane (Eastwood Lane), passing the remains of Eastwood Hall on your right. Just beyond

An impressive array of hand pumps in the Old Poets' Corner

the farm, take the signed footpath to your right, through a couple of squeezers, and then at 90 degrees left, keeping the hedge on your left, go straight down to emerge on the road by some houses (Hard Meadow Lane). Turn right here and you'll see a footpath sign pointing left about 200 yards ahead. Take this path through a couple of fields before bearing right on a well-worn track between two large trees. Now simply keep the field boundary closely on your right all the way into Ashover, past the sports ground, to emerge in the village right by the church and Crispin Inn. Go left downhill and at the bottom you'll find the **Old Poets' Corner 2**, formerly known as

the Red Lion. Under its new incarnation the Old Poets' Corner has become a real destination pub, offering a permanent mini beer festival from its eight handpumps (with a strong emphasis on beers from micro-breweries). Cider drinkers are also well catered for since the Poets is a former winner of the National CAMRA Cider Pub award, as well as being a local CAMRA Pub Of The Year. Excellent food (which has earned the Poets a place in CAMRA's *Good Pub Food* guide) is available lunchtimes and evenings with a Sunday carvery until 3pm. At the time of writing the pub was moving towards all-day opening (from noon) but it may be wise to phone ahead and check first if you're expecting to arrive during the afternoon. The pub also offers bed and breakfast and a holiday cottage (details on website). The interior of the pub is large and rambling and not without architectural interest. Note particularly the carved panelling and fireplace in the right hand room as you enter.

It can be all too easy to get too comfortable in here and forget that you need to get back to Matlock; if so you will certainly be envious of those who have decided to stay the night here or nearby.

PUB INFORMATION

1 Nettle Inn
Milltown, Ashover
Chesterfield, Derbyshire S45 0ES
01246 590642
Hours: 11-2.30, 5.30-11;
11-10.30 Sun
Food: lunchtimes and evenings

Local attractions: Matlock (see Walk 4), 4 miles; Chesterfield Museum, market and 'crooked spire' church, 6 miles; Crich Tramway Museum (www.tramway.co.uk), 6 miles; Wingfield Manor ruins (see www.english-heritage.org.uk), 6 miles.

2 Old Poets' Corner
Butts Road, Ashover
Chesterfield, Derbyshire S45 0EW
01246 590888
www.oldpoets.co.uk
Hours: 12.30-2.30, 5-11;
12-11 Fri-Sun
Food: lunchtimes and evenings

Handsome carved wooden fireplace in the Old Poets' Corner, Ashover

Arkwright's Cromford and Lea Green

WALK INFORMATION

Start/Finish: Cromford Market Place, by Greyhound Hotel (⊙ 296566)

Access: Transpeak Manchester-Nottingham service hourly, also R6.1 from Derby. Rail from Derby to Cromford Station on route ¼ mile into walk

Distance: 5 miles (8 km). OS Map: Explorer OL24

The walk: A circular route with one long, steep climb near the start but a relatively easy walk thereafter

The pubs: Jug & Glass Inn, Lea; Boat Inn, Bell Inn, both Cromford

A circular route leading from Richard Arkwright's famous industrial village into pleasant countryside and returning along the old Cromford Canal, with plenty of interest, including links with another two historic figures. Plan to leave Cromford at about 10.30am in order to make best use of the opening times at the Jug & Glass, or even earlier if you need to fill up at the Tor Café.

From industrial pioneer Arkwright's handsome Greyhound Hotel in Cromford's Market Place, walk down to the road junction and cross the A6 by the traffic lights to the Tor Café. A worthwhile stop if you have time to spare, this little gem – a favourite for cyclists – bills itself as the oldest café in the Peak District, and it's certainly the smallest. 50 yards left (north) from the Tor Café enter a concessionary path through stone pillars alongside the river Derwent. A beetling limestone crag towers over you on the right and ahead is St Mary's Parish Church, originally

View over Cromford, considered the 'Cradle of the Industrial Revolution'

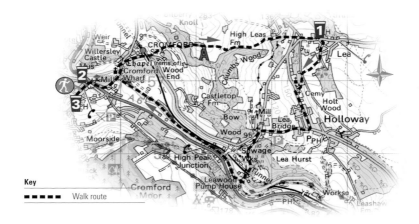

Key
■ ■ ■ ■ ■ Walk route

intended as a private chapel for Willersley Castle. Ignore the footpath (on the right) to the mill which we shall visit at the end, rejoin the road by the church and walk left, carefully crossing the handsome 15th-century bridge by a small fishing temple, identified by the inscription 'piscatoribus sacrum' (sacred to fishermen) in the stonework.

Willersley Castle, which would have been Sir Richard Arkwright's residence, had he lived long enough, is off to the left and offers teas and lunches to non-residents. Continue on the lower Lea Road past the impressive Cromford Bridge Hall, overlooking the meadows of the Derwent flood plain, to the railway bridge. (The

railway station, designed by Joseph Paxton's son-in-law in a striking Neo-Alpine style and immortalised by Oasis on a record cover is a minute's detour for railway fans.) 50 yards beyond the bridge, take the footpath as it heads off left (signed to Lea & Dethick), climbing steeply up to and over a stile. Pause here for the view behind you of the mill, Arkwright's home (Rock House) to the left, and the quarries above the village beyond. Onwards and upwards. Keep the wall on your right over the next stile and follow the path as it sticks close to the overhead telegraph wires. If you stop

The final resting place of Richard Arkwright, St Mary's Church, Cromford

to rest here you should be able to make out the chimney at Middleton Top at the start of the High Peak Trail (see Walk 7) – it's directly above the active quarry.

At the top of the climb you'll find a wider bridleway, Hearthstone Lane. You need to double back and left for about 30 yards to pick up the Lea path over a stile on the right (A, ⊙ 312574). That's the climbing over! In front of you the wide vista includes Lea village straight ahead, whilst the farmstead and church slightly to the left is Dethick. This little hamlet was the birthplace of Anthony Babington (1561–86) who was convicted of plotting the assassination of Elizabeth I and conspiring with the imprisoned Mary Queen of Scots. Mary's alleged involvement in the 'Babington Plot' led to her execution on grounds of treason. To your right, atop the quarry, is the famous landmark of Crich Stand, memorial to the Sherwood Foresters who died in WWI, with the village church's spire also visible. As you get lower see if you can pick out the castellated chimneys of Lea Green, once the home of industrialist John Smedley and now a Derbyshire County Council sports and activities centre. Lea, however, is associated more with Florence Nightingale (1820–1910), who spent her summers not at Lea Green but at Lea Hurst, the family estate in nearby Holloway to which she retired after her career.

Holloway is the large village you'll see on the hillside to your right as you walk downhill. Before you reach the lane at the bottom of the hill the path plunges unexpectedly through a pretty little holly and bluebell wood with a stream gurgling below. Cross this on stepping stones just before coming to the road. Go straight across and through an aptly named squeezer stile. Climb to another after 50 yards. At this one the latitudinally challenged may have problems and even be forced to retreat and go round via the road! Having emerged onto the second lane the sign of the **Jug & Glass Inn** 🚩 is visible

Stepping stones and stile at a pretty little stream near Lea Green

some 250 yards ahead beyond Lea Green Centre.

The Jug & Glass is a free house at the near end of a terrace of former weavers' cottages reputedly built by the uncle of Florence Nightingale. It has moved upmarket since the author visited it in the mid-70s as a student but still retains something of its former layout with wood-panelled rooms leading off a central servery. There is a newish restaurant at one extremity but drinkers are welcome and, indeed, the beer range is wide with Whim Hartington IPA and Black Sheep alongside other national brews, and a guest ale. The pub also runs a beer festival on the August Bank Holiday. Dogs are welcome, as are children in the restaurant at lunchtimes. Importantly the pub also offers

RICHARD ARKWRIGHT AND CROMFORD MILL

In August 1771 Richard Arkwright, having moved to Cromford from Lancashire and partnered with the Strutts of Belper, built the world's first successful water-powered cotton spinning mill here. It was arguably the beginning of the factory system, with a sizeable workforce, strict working hours and round-the-clock production. Later mills followed on this site and nearby at Masson Mill on the Derwent a few years later. Arkwright also built some high quality housing for his workers and created an early model village, which is largely intact today.

The importance of Sir Richard Arkwright's achievements here, and those of his partners, the Strutts, at Belper and elsewhere on the Derwent, was given the ultimate recognition in 2001 when UNESCO inscribed a 15-mile (24-km) stretch of the Derwent Valley between Matlock Bath as a World Heritage site.

Careful restoration of the buildings at Cromford continues under the guidance of the Arkwright Society after years of other industrial uses and later neglect. Rewarding tours of the site are available and guides in the shop give a far more comprehensive history of this fascinating site than is possible here.

Cromford centre, St Mary's Church and Cromford Bridge with Dene Quarry in the background

accommodation in five rooms and would make a good venue from which to explore the walks and pubs of this delightful corner of Derbyshire.

For a bus back to Lea Bridge or Matlock, walk down to Lea Common (best to ask for directions in the pub) to catch the 140/1 service – this runs

Worth a visit, the Jug & Glass Inn, Lea

hourly until early evening, then two later buses. Otherwise, leaving the pub take Holt Lane opposite that runs by the children's playground and then swings to the right after 50 yards. Carrying on, the road becomes a track at Holt House after another 100 yards (FP sign) and 75 yards beyond that a path, signed to Holloway, leads right and skirts around the wall of Lea Green Centre's grounds to emerge on a quiet lane. Cross this onto another path running through woodland with the squat tower of Holloway Church on your right. This brings you onto a lower road (Church Street). Turning left here after crossing affords good views down to the mills at Lea Bridge and up to the Black Rocks above Cromford.

The walk down Church Street to Lea Bridge is simple if unexciting: carry on to the end of this lane and turn right downhill, keeping a substantial wall on your right. At the end, close to the atmospheric John Smedley's mill, where the road to Lea and Riber heads off right, go left on a wide track (no sign) into Lea Wood which leads pleasantly down the abandoned Nightingale Arm of the Cromford Canal by Wharf cottage (note the circular metal old crane base in the stone setts on the wharf). The Nightingale family had a hatmaking factory on the modern Smedley mills' site. Beyond an impressive location where the railway crosses the river and then, underneath you, plunges immediately into a tunnel, you reach the Cromford Canal proper where the picturesque ruin before you is an old lengthsman's cottage (a lengthsman was responsible for the inspection and maintenance of a length

Lea Wood Pumping House, built to pump water from the Derwent to Cromford Canal

soldiered on until 1944. As yet it has not been restored to use.

There is plenty of interest as you turn right and stroll along the canal (do not cross). First up is the attractive Lea Wood Pumping House with its restored beam engine dating back to 1849, open free to the public at times. This huge engine, driven by two locomotive boilers, pumped nearly four tons of water per stroke into the canal to keep it navigable.

of canal). The canal was opened in 1793 to link Arkwright's Mills to the outside world, but was soon undermined by the railways, although it

Across the canal and a little further along is the old wharf shed for the High Peak Railway (see information box). It is remarkable to think that

THE CROMFORD AND HIGH PEAK RAILWAY

Built towards the end of the canal era and first conceived as a canal rather than a railway, the Cromford and High Peak Railway was considered to be an engineering masterpiece which attracted railway enthusiasts from all over the world. After the completion of the Peak Forest Canal in 1800, which had its terminus at Whaley Bridge, a number of ambitious but impractical schemes were devised to link it with the Cromford Canal. All were abandoned in favour of a railway, but as it was built by a canal engineer, Josiah Jessop, the stations were called 'wharfs' and the long level sections were interspersed with sharp inclines (instead of locks), the steepest of which were aided by stationary steam engines. The final cost was £180,000, more than Jessop's estimate of £155,000, but still much cheaper than a canal.

Opened as a horse-drawn railway and then converted to steam in 1831, it was thus one of the country's earliest railways. The railway was used to transport minerals, corn, coal and other vital commodities from the Cromford canal to the High Peak canal. Since the line had been built on the canal principle of following contours, there were many fairly tight curves, which in later years, were to hamper operations. Not only

did the Cromford and High Peak Railway (C&HPR) have the steepest unaided incline of any line in the country, the 1 in 14 of Hopton, it also had the sharpest curve, 55 yards through 80 degrees at Gotham. The line was isolated until 1853 when, in an effort to improve traffic, a connection was made with the Manchester, Buxton, Matlock and Midlands Junction Railway at High Peak Junction just north of Whatstandwell. However, the line never achieved a profit and fell victim to Dr Richard Beeching's cuts and shut in 1967.

A few years later and the C&HPR was (and remains) back in business as a popular 17-mile leisure trail for cyclists, walkers and horse riders.

High Peak Junction Workshops at the start of the High Peak Trail

Pretty mixed woodland surroundings near the Canal Wharf, Cromford

until about 40 years ago the railway was still in regular use and was connected to the Derby line a little to the south of this point. Just beyond is High Peak Junction itself at the foot of a long and steep incline which carried the old railway on to the plateau and eventually across to Whaley Bridge. The workshops across the bridge house a small but interesting display of tools and other railway artifacts – worth a visit, if open.

From here it is a pleasant and easy one-mile stroll back along the canal to Cromford. If you're waiting for opening time, the café at Wheatcroft Wharf makes a pleasant stop, and of course a visit to Arkwright's mill across the road is highly recommended. Five minutes' walk up Mill Road beyond the mill to the left sees you back at the Tor Café and central Cromford, where the **Boat Inn** 2 and the **Bell Inn** 3 may attract your attention (for pub descriptions see Walk 4: Matlock to Cromford via Lumsdale and Bonsall).

PUB INFORMATION

1 Jug & Glass Inn
Main Road, Lea
Matlock, Derbyshire DE4 5GJ
01629 534232
Hours: 12-2 (not Mon), 7-11 (not Sun)
Food: lunchtime and evenings until 9pm; Sunday lunch carvery

2 Boat Inn
Scarthin, Cromford
Matlock, Derbyshire DE4 3QF
01629 823282
Hours: 12-3, 6-11; 12-3, 7-11 Sat; 12-3, 7-10.30 Sun
Food: lunchtimes and evenings

3 Bell Inn
47 Cromford Hill, Cromford
Matlock, Derbyshire DE4 3RF
01629 822102
Hours: 7-11; 12-3, 7-11 Sat; 12-3, 7-10.30 Sun
No food available

Local attractions: Lea Rhododendron Gardens (www.leagarden.co.uk); Cromford Mill; Crich Tramway Village with working trams (www.tramway.co.uk), 3 miles.

Traditional wrought-iron pub sign at Lea's Jug & Glass Inn

Black Rocks and the High Peak Trail from Wirksworth

WALK INFORMATION

Start/Finish: Wirksworth Market Place

Access: Bus service R6.1 from Derby. Nearest rail station at Cromford, 2 miles

Distance: 4 miles (6.5 km). OS Map: Explorer OL24

The walk: A moderately difficult circular walk with one steep climb. Not recommended for families

The pubs: Black's Head, Royal Oak, both Wirksworth

A circular route from Wirksworth, known for its lead mining and limestone quarrying. Once Derbyshire's second town, this 18th-century boom town had fallen into decay by the 1950s and remained so until a regeneration project in 1978 rescued many of its fine old buildings from ruin and the town received a conservation award five years later. Today it's a lively spot with successful businesses and a summer arts festival. The walk's key attractions include no less than three old railways, the National Stone Centre and the start of the Pennine Bridleway along with some stunning views. A steep climb up to Black Rocks makes this route moderate in terms of difficulty, but navigation is straightforward. Note that *Good Beer Guide* regular the Royal Oak is closed lunchtimes except for Sunday and that neither of the pubs on this route are suitable for children.

View over Wirksworth's rooftops, nestled into the surrounding hills

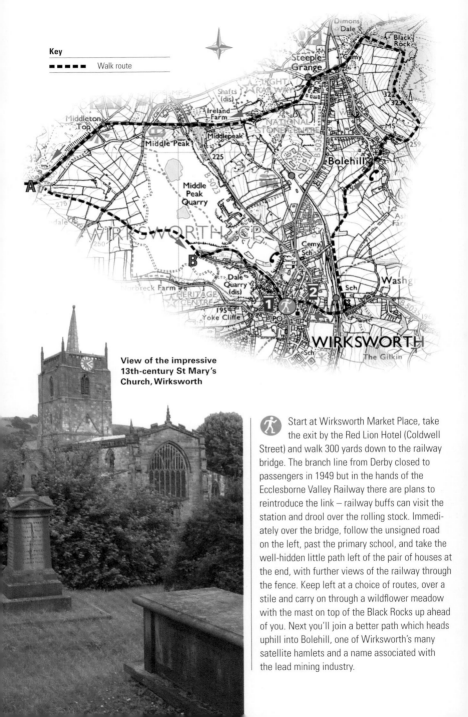

Key

■ ■ ■ ■ ■ Walk route

View of the impressive
13th-century St Mary's
Church, Wirksworth

Start at Wirksworth Market Place, take
the exit by the Red Lion Hotel (Coldwell
Street) and walk 300 yards down to the railway
bridge. The branch line from Derby closed to
passengers in 1949 but in the hands of the
Ecclesborne Valley Railway there are plans to
reintroduce the link – railway buffs can visit the
station and drool over the rolling stock. Immediately over the bridge, follow the unsigned road
on the left, past the primary school, and take the
well-hidden little path left of the pair of houses at
the end, with further views of the railway through
the fence. Keep left at a choice of routes, over a
stile and carry on through a wildflower meadow
with the mast on top of the Black Rocks up ahead
of you. Next you'll join a better path which heads
uphill into Bolehill, one of Wirksworth's many
satellite hamlets and a name associated with
the lead mining industry.

As you cross the road uphill past the old chapel, the gradient gets more serious – this is probably the toughest part of the route. Carry on across another lane, then follow the path as it ducks left (signed) into a narrow alley between gardens, still very steep, until you emerge breathlessly on the top road where a well earned rest might be in order. Turn right on the road for about 100 yards and at the bend cross with care to take the signed path up onto the open hillside flanking Black Rocks. The 'no cycles' sign seems superfluous! Views are every bit as good as they ought to be for the effort you've expended.

Head into the trees again on a well signed route that takes you to the white concrete trig point at the summit. Here you've pretty much a 360 degree panorama.

The ultra-traditional Royal Oak in Wirksworth is a Good Beer Guide regular on account of its excellent ales

Look west to Carsington Reservoir and Middleton Top Engine House with the National Stone Centre below. To the northeast is Matlock with the folly of Riber Castle also visible. Hardest to spot, further right, through the trees, is the beacon on Crich Stand, above the National Tramway Museum.

Start down the well-worn track and follow the twists and turns through pleasant mixed woodland. As you pass Black Rocks proper you get an unwelcome view of the gigantic Dene Quarry ahead – one of the Peak's largest active workings. Peak quarries are often well hidden but this time you get a real eyeful. Join the High Peak Trail (for information on this old railway route see Walk 6) and follow it left for about a mile up to the visitor centre at Middleton Top. On the way you'll pass the Steeple Grange Light Railway, another old quarry route, and the new(ish) National Stone Centre in another old quarry to your left. One of the highlights at the Centre is a fascinating outdoor collection of stretches of dry stone walling in styles from all over Great Britain, built by the respective groups of the Drystone Walling Association – a great free show. The relatively steep pull on the route here is the Middleton Incline, one of several which employed cables to haul railway wagons uphill – the wayside information boards

Perfect walking terrain, the thickly wooded High Peak Trail at the Middleton Incline

The High Peak Trail near Middleton, a popular route for walkers, riders and cyclists

tell a more detailed story of these and other sights. The visitor centre at Middleton Top has a selection of guides, and a refreshment vending machine (please check in advance for opening times). Beyond the engine house, bear left after 450 yards at the first gate (A, ⊙ 271548) and take a signed path bearing left again under telegraph wires using the masts on a hilltop ahead as a rough guide. Walk on through some squeezer stiles and flower meadows and over a minor road for more of the same.

The next section of the route is rather messy. The path has been diverted from the line of the route shown on the Ordnance Map as the quarry has expanded. You should be able to follow the new route which currently heads across a disused part of the quarry, not a pretty sight but it's soon over, and you emerge on a sharp bend of a quiet lane, once more in a pleasant, wooded setting (B, ⊙ 281544). Take the left-hand path heading slightly uphill for some

excellent views across the town as you return towards Wirksworth. The lane, Greenhill, leads steeply down into town. If you've time to spare, the little alleyways ('ginnels' in the local parlance) off to the right of the lane offer an alternative way down to the Market Place.

The **Black's Head** **1** on the Market Place is a very handsome brick-built former Kimberley pub, which at the time of writing hadn't succumbed to the generic pub sign frenzy of Greene King, although perhaps ironically the original sign has been replaced by a Saracen, no doubt in the interests of modern sensitivities. 'Blackamoor's Head' was once a common pub name, and the term 'Blackamoor' appears in Shakespeare. It's likely that it derives from the Mauri tribe whence Mauritania is named. A small but cosy interior awaits, and there's a tiny patio garden. Four beers from the Greene King stable are on tap, together with a good range of sandwiches and meals most sessions. There are other eating options around the Market Place.

The **Royal Oak** **2** is Wirksworth's *Good Beer Guide* regular. To find it, head down Coldwell Street for the second time, but take the street on your left (North End) and you'll see the sign in the centre of a handsome stone terrace as you turn in. A well-run, slightly old-fashioned (and nothing wrong with that!) adult drinking environment, with Draught Bass a regular, and three other skilfully kept ales usually featuring Taylor Landlord and a Whim beer.

PUB INFORMATION

1 **Black's Head**
Market Place, Wirksworth
Matlock, Derbyshire DE4 4ET
01629 823257
Hours: 12-2, 5.30-11; 12-midnight Sat; 12-3, 7-11 Sun
Food: sandwiches and meals available most sessions

2 **Royal Oak**
North End, Wirksworth
Matlock, Derbyshire DE4 4FG
01629 823000
Hours: 8-11.30 (midnight Fri & Sat); 12-3, 7.30-11 Sun

Local attractions: Wirksworth Heritage Centre; Ecclesbourne Valley Railway; National Stone Centre, ½ mile; Carsington Reservoir, 4 miles; Arkwright's Mill, Cromford, 2 miles.

The Black's Head in a corner of Wirksworth Market Place

bakewell group

above: **Monsal Dale** below: **Gardens at Alport**

Youlgrave and the Lathkill and Bradford Rivers

WALK INFORMATION

Start/Finish: The bridge at Alport, near Youlgrave (⊙ 222646)

Access: To Bakewell via Transpeak Manchester-Nottingham service or Trent Barton bus number 6.1 from Derby, then local bus service Hulleys 171. Hulleys 172 from Matlock Bus Station

Distance: 5¼ miles (8.5 km) returning via Youlgrave. OS Map: Explorer OL 24

The walk: Easy-to-follow circular route between two (or more) good pubs. One steep climb

The pubs: George Hotel, Youlgrave; Lathkil Hotel, Over Haddon. Option to visit the Bull's Head Hotel, Youlgrave

The pure waters of the Lathkill and the Bradford have cut deep valleys north and south of the large and popular village of Youlgrave notable for one of the biggest and most impressive churches in the Peak District. The streams have their confluence at Alport where this walk starts. The paths on the route are well-signed and well-walked allowing you to enjoy the excellent scenery. There is one stiff climb (on tarmac) up to Over Haddon. You're never far from a top-notch pub or two, and the all day opening of the George allows for some flexibility in the timing.

At the tiny hamlet of Alport, long ago bypassed by the main road, it's worth delaying your start for a few minutes and appreciating the setting at the bridge over the River Bradford. It's an idyllic spot where you may be lucky enough to see the colourful flash of a kingfisher. Just downstream of the bridge is an old lead smelter, one of many in this area; adjacent is an ore crusher with its mill wheel.

Stone cottages by the River Bradford at Alport

The walk is clearly signposted

Key

▬ ▬ ▬ ▬ Walk route

• • • • • Detour

Pretty gardens lining the river at Alport

Head the other way (southwest) along the lane between the picturebook houses and their charming riverside gardens, past impressive Monks Hall just before the lane reaches the main road. Bear left by the phone box and the bridge, from where you can see below the confluence of

the Bradford and the Lathkill, two of Derbyshire's purest freshwater streams. Head left again immediately down a wide track, which leads you along the pretty River Bradford, one of the most attractive short riverside walks in the county.

Everything is on a small scale here, from the stream to the little crags on your left. Look out for the impressive Youlgrave church tower which comes into view on your right, and shortly afterwards, cross the tiny humpback bridge over the stream and follow the narrower track to Mawstone Lane and straight ahead into the heart of Youlgrave, to All Saints' Parish Church and the **George Hotel** 🔳.

Youlgrave is a large linear village that is well worth a closer look – it still has 'real' shops, three pubs, a youth hostel and other signs of the vibrancy that has disappeared from many villages. The George should be open when you arrive, and if it isn't my advice is to wait until it is, unless you intend to visit at the end of the walk (see below). It retains its three-room internal layout; many locals prefer the back room, but the front has a traditional public bar complete with terrazzo floor and red leatherette benches, which shouldn't be missed. The well-kept beers from the Scottish & Newcastle portfolio include Theakston's Mild. The pub is a real village hub that, following the demise of the village chippy, even offers take-away fish and chips.

The church is worth a look too: the wide nave contains three bay arcades, and an impressive circular font with some animal motifs, dating from around 1200, that was once in Elton's church. It also has some interesting tombs. The church was substantially restored around 1870.

The walk continues westwards up Church Street to the *Bull's Head Hotel* (a handsome Marston's house that may be worth a visit on the way home); immediately beyond, by the youth hostel and the distinctive old well (the village is well-known for its annual well dressings towards the end of June) fork right into Moor Lane past the Old Hall and up the hill. A few minutes up the rise, after a bend, take the track to the right which climbs gently giving wide views across to Stanton Moor (with radio mast), while below you the wooded valley of the Lathkill is visible. The track becomes a footpath and Over Haddon village is visible ahead of you (the distinctive white building is the next goal). Cross over a minor lane and bear slightly to the right. The path shortly descends to the agricultural hamlet of

**The village of Over Haddon
and the River Lathkill**

LEAD MINING IN LATHKILL DALE

Lathkill Dale may seem silent today but there's plenty of evidence of past industry. A significant legacy is some pillars from a large aqueduct (fed from a channel or 'goyt' which runs parallel to the river further upstream). This was used to drive a large 50-ft waterwheel that drained lead mines in and around the valley. Soughs are drains which ran almost horizontally from underneath lead workings which had reached down to the water table. They were used to drain water out into a stream so that mining could continue. The River Lathkill itself was straightened and its bed lined with clay to prevent water penetrating the workings. Near the aqueduct is the restored ruin of Bateman's House, home of James Bateman, the agent for Lathkill Mines in the 1840s, and built directly over a deep lead mineshaft. The building has recently been made safe and can be explored.

An old lead smelter, Alport

Meadow Place Grange snugly tucked into a fold of the landscape. Enjoy the quietly decaying yet excellent collection of farm buildings set around a yard whilst you can, since it surely will soon be turned into yet another holiday complex.

Walk through the yard on the same trajectory and then, bearing ever so slightly right, head

View over the Lathkill towards Youlgrave

Public bar of the George Hotel, Youlgrave

across a field and suddenly you're at the top brink of the valley of the Lathkill, which cuts steeply into the limestone at this point. Travel through the gate to the right and down to a pleasant clapper bridge at as gentle an angle as the terrain permits. The Lathkill (see information box) is a National Nature Reserve and, if you have time, the permissive footpath left following the river upstream is thoroughly recommended. The tranquillity belies a lively industrial past. From here it's a short but punishingly steep pull up the quiet zigzagging lane into Over Haddon; keep bearing right as you walk through the village which will bring you unerringly to the penultimate building, the **Lathkil Hotel 2**. Architecturally nothing of real interest remains and visually it's no oil painting but this must be one of the finest views from a Peakland pub, across the meadows and valley towards Youlgrave. Beer-wise too this is a pub of superlatives which camps out permanently in the *Good Beer Guide*.

There is an excellent choice of ales on tap with local micros like Whim (Hartington) well represented, and plenty of food. For children, a family room is available at lunchtimes.

Leaving the pub head left to the end of the lane and you'll find a footpath leading to the right across worn grass (aim slightly to the left of Youlgrave church tower) and on over the meadow, keeping on a shelf above the valley and passing through a couple of stiles. A superb view of the river in its valley opens up to your right before you cross another stile forking right to keep just above the steep slopes. This leads down to a small road (Shutts Lane) just above Conksbury bridge (A, ◉ 212657). Drop down to the bridge, an attractive spot, but don't be fooled by the 'Quiet Lane' signs as this road is a real rural rat-run, particularly for rush-hour traffic. About 150 yards up the other side, turn left onto a footpath that follows the river downstream. At Raper Lodge (B, ◉ 214651) after another 500 yards you can either continue ahead along the river valley to reach Alport in 10 minutes, or turn up the tiny, tarred lane (Coalpit Lane) to reach Youlgrave in a similar time and revisit the George at your leisure. In this case return to Alport the way you came in.

PUB INFORMATION

1 George Hotel
Main Street
Youlgrave, Derbyshire
DE45 1VW
01629 636292
Hours: 11-11; 12-10.30 Sun
Food: 11.30-9; 12-8 Sun

2 Lathkil Hotel
School Lane, Over Haddon
Bakewell, Derbyshire DE45 1JE
01629 812501
Hours: 11.30-3, 6.30-11; 11.30-11 Sat; 12-10.30 Sun
Food: lunchtimes and evenings (booking recommended in evening)

TRY ALSO:

Bull's Head Hotel
Fountain Square, Church Street
Youlgrave, Derbyshire DE45 1UR
01629 636307
www.bullsheadyoulgrave.co.uk
Hours: 11.30-2.30 (4 Sat & Sun), 6.30-midnight (1am Thu-Sat)
Food: all sessions except Monday lunch

Local attractions: Lathkill Dale National Nature Reserve; Arbor Low Henge, 3 miles; Chatsworth, 4 miles; Haddon Hall, 2 miles; Caudwell's Mill and Craft Museum, 3 miles; Bakewell, historic market town, 3 miles.

NOTICE TO ALL VAGABOND
FOUND LODGING LOITERING O
BEGGING WITHIN THIS HAMLI
WILL BE TAKEN UP AND DEA
WITH AS THE LAW DIRECT

A stern warning in Alport

Stanton Moor from Rowsley

WALK INFORMATION

Start/Finish: Peacock Hotel, Rowsley – on A6 between Matlock and Bakewell (⊙ 257658)

Access: Transpeak Manchester–Nottingham service hourly, also R6.1 from Derby

Distance: 4¾ miles (7½ km) (1 mile extra with recommended Stanton Moor extension). OS Map: Explorer OL24

The walk: A varied circular route, with optional detour onto Stanton Moor and links to Walk 8

The pub: Flying Childers Inn, Stanton-in-Peak

A varied circuit full of interest combining Derwent Valley views and the atmospheric Stanton Moor, a gritstone island in the White Peak and renowned for its stone circle. There are well-signed paths and the terrain is straightforward with only short very steep sections. The route can be taken in both directions but the pub is only open for two hours at lunchtime, and closed Monday and Tuesday lunchtimes, so plan ahead! Allow about two hours for the clockwise circuit to the pub including time on Stanton Moor, and around an hour for the anti-clockwise route via Congreave. Those wanting to make a very full day of it can link the walk to the Youlgrave circuit (Walk 8).

Darley Dale viewed from Stanton Moor

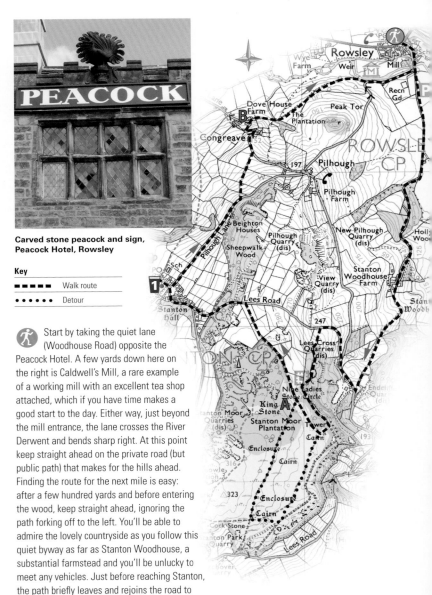

Carved stone peacock and sign,
Peacock Hotel, Rowsley

Key

▪▪▪▪▪ Walk route

●●●●●● Detour

Start by taking the quiet lane (Woodhouse Road) opposite the Peacock Hotel. A few yards down here on the right is Caldwell's Mill, a rare example of a working mill with an excellent tea shop attached, which if you have time makes a good start to the day. Either way, just beyond the mill entrance, the lane crosses the River Derwent and bends sharp right. At this point keep straight ahead on the private road (but public path) that makes for the hills ahead. Finding the route for the next mile is easy: after a few hundred yards and before entering the wood, keep straight ahead, ignoring the path forking off to the left. You'll be able to admire the lovely countryside as you follow this quiet byway as far as Stanton Woodhouse, a substantial farmstead and you'll be unlucky to meet any vehicles. Just before reaching Stanton, the path briefly leaves and rejoins the road to avoid a zigzag bend. Keep straight through the buildings; the view beyond is of Stanton Moor, and, in fact, ahead of you in the trees you should be able to pick out a tower at the edge of the moor, which we will visit shortly. Until 2007, determined eco-warriors campaigned for many years to prevent the re-opening of the Endcliffe Quarry near the top end of this path, which would have had a disastrous effect upon Stanton Moor. It now looks as if their efforts have been rewarded and if all is quiet when you pass, make a note to raise your first glass later on to toast all their hard work.

The slowly dilapidating Earl Grey Tower, on the northern edge of Stanton Moor

STANTON MOOR'S HISTORY

There are many prehistoric remains on Stanton Moor but the Nine Ladies stone circle is probably the best known. The circle was probably a sacred site where religious ceremonies took place, not just for Bronze Age burial purposes but for celebrations as well. The circle is 33 ft in diameter and about 130 ft away stands another stone, the King's Stone (only revealed in the 1970s after droughts and soil erosion). Legend has it that nine ladies and a fiddler were turned to stone for making music and dancing on the Sabbath.

On reaching the quiet road (Lees Road) bear right again, take the left fork after a couple of minutes and then, after following the road uphill and around to the left, look for a signed footpath on your left. Take this path across a field, through a broken metal gate and then join a curving path around to the right of a copse of trees and follow this steadily but not too steeply uphill on to Stanton Moor itself. As the path bears left a little, you'll notice the change in scenery as the rock beneath your feet changes from limestone to sandstone. Soon you arrive at the square Earl Grey Tower built by the Thornhill family of Stanton to commemorate the passing of the Reform Bill of 1832. There are fine views out across the Derwent Valley towards Matlock. If time presses, head straight across to the Nine Ladies stone circle just a couple of minutes away uphill by climbing over the stile and heading more or less directly away from it. The stone circle will soon appear but don't expect Stonehenge: they're only about 18 inches tall! (A, 🔘 249635).
If you have half an hour or so to spare I strongly recommend an extended stroll around the open moor, for this is a special place with a distinctive landscape very different to most of the White

Peak. Continue along the edge of the moor from the Earl Grey Tower without crossing the fence, enjoying the extensive views, for over 10 minutes until you reach and cross a stile by a pedestal rock outcrop. Take the path heading away from here until you reach another path crossing at right angles. Turn right here and you should be back by the standing stones in another 10 minutes, suitably invigorated by the heathland walk. As a guide for the walk back to the Nine Ladies, the tall white mast on the moor should be in front and to the left of you. From Nine Ladies head north (or bear right if coming from the tower) on a good path over a stile back into an enclosed landscape and down to the minor road (Lees Road). Here simply turn left and

The shady path on the link route to Alport

walk down the road into Stanton-in-Peak beyond the church, arriving, if possible, at noon when the bolts slide back at the **Flying Childers Inn** [1]. The pub, named after an 18th-century racehorse, is a pleasantly unpretentious local, especially given the well-heeled village in which it lies. The domestic origins of the building can be discerned from the exterior, with bricked up doorways and all. William Thornhill, an erstwhile occupant of Stanton Hall, has his initials carved above the entrance. There are two rooms, including an excellent public bar with benches and open fire. Even the disused old off-sales hatch is still there between the two bars. Although the pub now serves Black Sheep Bitter and Wells' Bombardier plus a guest ale, the guv'nor has retained some old Wards of Sheffield memorabilia in the shape of some badged glasses and a sign above the servery. Food is appropriately simple, crusty rolls (called cobs and filled with tender roast meats on Sunday) and sandwiches with soup.

If you want to make a day of your pub trail, follow the link to Alport and the start of the Youlgrave circuit (about 1½ miles) at the end of this section. Otherwise, leaving the pub retrace your steps to the road junction just beyond the church and head left along Pilhough Lane, with fine views across another section of the Derwent Valley. After about 10 minutes you'll reach a stile on your left. Before crossing the stile and descending downhill, see if you can identify the solid church tower at Youlgrave, towards the left of the vista, and then in the valley itself the castellations of Haddon Hall, with the spire of Bakewell church beyond. Haddon Hall is the home of the Manners family (a seat of the Duke of Rutland), and is one of the finest medieval and Tudor houses in England. Now the path drops steeply down through pasture to another lane via a stile. Here turn left and continue dropping steeply as its zigzags through the tiny hamlet of Congreave. Just as the bends straighten

The Flying Childers Inn, Stanton-in-Peak, created out of several 18th-century cottages

take a path to your right (B, ⊙ 246654) which leads across the fields in and out of a small clough (steep valley) and then more gently down towards Rowsley, the last stretch on a quiet lane (Peaktor Lane), before turning left into Woodhouse Road into Rowsley to the starting point.

If you are later starting from Rowsley it may make more sense to do this route in reverse. Route finding should present no particular difficulties: take care when walking after leaving Stanton tower to drop down to the road at the end of the wooded stretch and not be drawn into the curving track staying in the trees.

Link to Alport: A fairly easy downhill stroll of little more than half an hour. Walk down the road from the pub for about 300 yards and take a path right opposite a lodge. This route follows a wonderful tree-shaded course down to the B5056 road by the lower Lathkill River. Here walk back up the road to the left for about 275 yards and take the lane right, which climbs uphill for a bit past Harthill Hall. Look for a footpath sign off to the right through a caravan park and then dramatically down a steep brae to land you in the charming riverside hamlet of Alport. You'll be pleased to know that the George in Youlgrave is open all day!

PUB INFORMATION

[1] **Flying Childers Inn**
Main Road, Stanton-in-Peak
Matlock, Derbyshire DE4 2LW
01629 636333
Hours: 12-2 (not Mon-Tue, 3 Sat & Sun), 7-11 (10.30 Sun)
Food: lunchtimes only
Children in lounge bar only
CAMRA Regional Inventory

Local attractions: Chatsworth, 2 miles; Haddon Hall, 2 miles; Caudwell's Mill & Craft Museum; Peak Rail preservation group, Matlock to Rowsley (www.peakrail.co.uk); Red House Stables Carriage Museum, Darley Dale (www.workingcarriages.com), 2 miles; Bakewell, historic town, 3 miles.

Monsal Head Circuit via Litton

WALK INFORMATION

Start/Finish: Monsal Head Hotel (◎ 185715)

Access: Bus service Hulley's 173, Castleton-Tideswell-Bakewell, daily

Distance: 6 miles (9½ km) to the Three Stags' Heads; 9¾ miles (15½ km) for full round. OS Map: Explorer OL24

The walk: A scenic circular route that offers a snapshot of the best of the Peak District

The pubs: Red Lion Inn, Litton; Three Stags' Heads, Wardlow Mires; Monsal Head Hotel (Stables Bar), Monsal Head

If you had to choose just one walk to undertake, then I think this should be the one! It has everything you could want: great riverside paths, dry valleys, open views and natural history – and some of the widest beer choice you'll find in the Peak. The paths are well-walked, navigation is generally straightforward and the route is not unduly strenuous. Warning: after heavy rain the riverside path from Cressbrook Mill to Litton Mill can become flooded – an alternative high-level path avoids this stretch and is indicated in the text.

Start at Monsal Head, which is one of the best-known viewpoints in the National Park. Below you the River Wye curves round in a deep valley underneath the viaduct of the old Derby to Manchester railway. It's a bit of a visitor honeypot, but deservedly so. Head off opposite the recently refurbished café taking the path signed for the viaduct. You'll drop down though the woods and arrive close to the old tunnel portal. On the viaduct itself you'll find a quote from John Ruskin, an early environ-

View from Monsal Head over the disused viaduct crossing the River Wye

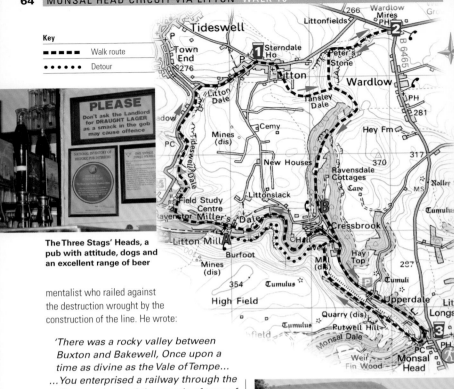

The Three Stags' Heads, a pub with attitude, dogs and an excellent range of beer

mentalist who railed against the destruction wrought by the construction of the line. He wrote:

'There was a rocky valley between Buxton and Bakewell, Once upon a time as divine as the Vale of Tempe...
...You enterprised a railway through the valley, you heaped thousands of tons of shale into its lovely stream; the valley is gone and the gods with it; and now every fool in Buxton can be at Bakewell in half an hour, and every fool in Bakewell at Buxton, which you think a lucrative process of exchange, you fools everywhere!'

The line closed in 1968 and today the silent, graceful arches of the viaduct actually seem to enhance the natural scenery.

Follow the trail for about a mile to Cressbrook where another tunnel blocks the old line so the trail veers off right through a gate with a view of Cressbrook Mill below. The present building was built in 1815 by William Newton who also dammed the river above Cressbrook to create the broad expanse of Water-cum-Jolly Dale, in effect the mill pond. It was derelict for years but has now, controversially maybe, been revamped as upmarket apartments. After 100 yards the path splits. If following the higher route due to

Tideswell Dale, a Wildlife Nature Reserve

wet conditions, keep on the high level track with good views across the valley. This route deposits you back on the railway track beyond the tunnel and close to Litton Mill, which is then reached by dropping to the river and crossing a footbridge soon after rejoining the old trackbed. Assuming good weather, take the low road and you'll reach the river at Water-cum-Jolly by an impressive weir which holds back the river in a wide pond. Cross the footbridge, and your route now heads left over a second footbridge across the old mill race to Cressbrook Mill.

A few yards along the path to the right, close to the new flats and in an interesting folly, is D's Brew Stop, a pleasantly unpretentious little tea room which I recommend (no toilets). Retrace those few yards to take the river path upstream through one of the most beautiful riverside miles in England, between the Wye and high limestone cliffs. You emerge at Litton Mill, another old industrial hamlet and scene of another apartment conversion whose affluence jars with the surroundings. This notorious mill was once the scene of some of the worst child labour excesses in the land [see information box].

Beyond the mill (the path from the high level detour rejoins here via a footbridge over the river), (A, ⊙ 159730) and 100 yards beyond the terrace of houses, a wide signed path takes you into charming Tideswell Dale enclosed by the limestone flanks which inspired the young David Bellamy on his visits to Ravenstor Youth Hostel above (once the mill owner's house). When you emerge at the top of the dale, by the car park and toilets, the path follows the roadside first though a fine avenue of beech trees and then over a paddock of Access Land as far as the junction with the Litton Road. Turning right here there's no alternative but to walk along the lane for about half a mile into the village.

Here, occupying an enviable position right on the green, you'll find the **Red Lion Inn** **1**, a rare instance of a licensed restaurant that has reverted to a proper pub – and a very good one too. It's full of character with a multi-roomed interior, sensible stone floors and welcoming open fires, all of which have helped to restore the pubby atmosphere. The menu is extensive and

WORKING IN LITTON MILL 1849

Accounts published in the Ashton Chronicle in 1849 tell of how seven- or eight-year-old boys and girls were taken from London workhouses and apprenticed in Cressbrook and Litton Mill. Children attempting to leave these places were imprisoned in the House of Correction. The working hours of these child slaves were from before five in the morning until nine or ten at night, with no time allowed away for meals.

Robert Blincoe, an orphan who managed to escape the mills, wrote in his memoirs: '... Ellis Needham, the master, had five sons, Frank, Charles, Samuel, Robert and John. These young men, particularly Frank and Charles, used us very cruelly, together with a man named Swann, an overlooker. They used to go up and down the mill with hazel sticks, out of the wood, and lay on us most unmercifully. Frank once beat me till he was frightened himself. He thought he had killed me. He had struck me on the temples and knocked me senseless. I was a long time before I came to myself again. Swann had a stick about two feet long with a pin or needle filed at the end of it, and would come slyly behind us, and run it into the thigh or any other part of the body, when we were not thinking about it. He once knocked me down and belaboured me with a thick stick over the head and face, cursing me in the most horrid way. To save my head I raised my arm, which he then bent with all his might. My elbow was broken. I bear the marks, and suffer pain from it to this day, and always shall as long as I live. The bone was fractured, but never had any notice taken of it. It was very seldom that we missed a day without being beaten in the most cruel and wanton manner...'

Impressive drystone wallscape near Litton

The fire in the ancient range at the Three Stags' Heads is always ablaze for visitors...

the food excellent, much locally sourced. Drinkers are also well-catered for with Oakwell Barnsley Bitter and Whim Hartington Bitter as regulars. Expect two other ever-changing guest beers. In good weather one can sit outside on the green alongside the village stocks.

Moving on, walk about 200 yards up the road (Church Lane) and look for a footpath sign pointing across the road to a step stile. Cross the road and stile into a meadow and follow the well-marked route across a walled track and down into the deep Tansley Dale, part of Cressbrook Dale National Nature Reserve. This is quintessential limestone country with grey walls dividing pasture in a classic Derbyshire enclosure landscape. Reach the main dale where, if it's been wet and the valley has a stream, you'll welcome the stepping stones. Here turn left and it's less than a mile up the beautiful valley past the striking Peter's Stone (the best views are enjoyed some time after you've passed beneath it) to Wardlow Mires, a tiny hamlet on the busy A623 where you'll find the **Three Stags' Heads** **2**, although it's only open at weekends. The Stags is a pub with attitude and loads of character, which you have to take on its terms. It's been carefully restored by owners Pat and Geoff Fuller who offer

home-cooked food served on plates made by Geoff in the adjacent workshop. The excellent ales on four handpumps, are from Abbeydale of Sheffield. One warning: this is an exceptionally dog-friendly pub and lurchers lie scattered around the two atmospheric rooms. One of England's classic pubs without a doubt!

There are occasional buses (route 173) that ply down the B-road almost opposite the pub back to Monsal Head (consult your public transport timetable carefully); otherwise the walk back takes us through pretty Cressbrook Dale. Retrace your route to the point where the stepping stones brought you into the valley bottom; from here a path, not shown on the OS map, leads along the valley southwards through quite dense scrub, but the walk is very rewarding – it feels like a little lost kingdom in here. It's easier to keep in the valley bottom at the footbridge, past Ravensdale cottages to eventually emerge on a quiet road (B, 172733). Walking down the little lane back to Cressbrook Mill is a matter of a few minutes, and then you can either retrace your steps to Monsal Head by turning right at the Mill, or continue along the pleasant little lane about a mile (past the hamlet of Uppermill) and up the hill to the Monsal Head Hotel. Alongside the hotel stands the **Stables Bar** **3**. It's a good conversion with the old horse stalls still evident and offers one of the best choices of well-kept real ales in the Peak, with a laudable commitment to local breweries. If the weather's good you can sit on the patio and enjoy the view with a nice pint. Food is available in the hotel.

PUB INFORMATION

1 **Red Lion Inn**
Main Street, Litton
Buxton, Derbyshire SK17 8QU
01298 871458
Hours: 12-3, 6-11; 12-11 Fri & Sat;
12-10.30 Sun
Food: available all sessions

2 **Three Stags' Heads**
Wardlow Mires, Buxton
Derbyshire SK17 8RW
01298 872268
Hours: 7-11 Fri; 12-11 Sat;
12-10.30 Sun
Food: available (please ring for times)

3 **Monsal Head Hotel**
(Stables Bar)
Monsal Head, Bakewell
Derbyshire DE45 1NL
01629 640250
www.monsalhead.com
Hours: 12-11 daily
Food: 12-9.30 (9 Sun)

Local attractions: Monsal Trail Path; Tideswell Village and 'Cathedral of the Peak', 1 mile; Eyam Plague Village, 5 miles; Chatsworth House and Gardens, 6 miles.

The White Peak Three-Village Circular

WALK INFORMATION

Start: Red Lion, Birchover – although other starting points en route are possible

Access: Bus service Hulley's 172 (not Sunday). Nearest rail station Matlock

Distance: 3¾ miles (6 km). OS Map: Explorer OL24

The walk: A fairly easy, well-signed and undulating walk with no extreme gradients

The pubs: Duke of York Inn, Elton; Old Bowling Green, Winster; Red Lion Inn, Birchover. Option to try Miners' Standard, Winster

Valley view near Winster looking to Birchover

In this well-walked part of the National Park the undulating topography makes for a very varied terrain in a small area. All three villages owe their existence at least in part to lead mining. The pubs are all very different, and you might like to adjust your starting point depending on personal preferences and starting time. The terrain is easy to moderate, and the paths well signed. Be aware that the wonderful Duke of York at Elton only opens at lunchtime on Sunday so despite the lack of public transport it's a good day to do this pleasant walk (the nearby Elton Café is also open on Sunday).

🚶 There is a logic to starting the walk at Birchover since the leg to Elton is the longest of the three and the Duke of York's lunchtime opening hours are the most restricted. You shouldn't miss the Red Lion (with its very distinctive sign) on Birchover's main street: from there stroll downhill for 100 yards to the Druid Inn (more of a restaurant than a pub these days) where the main road turns sharp right. Don't follow it but con-

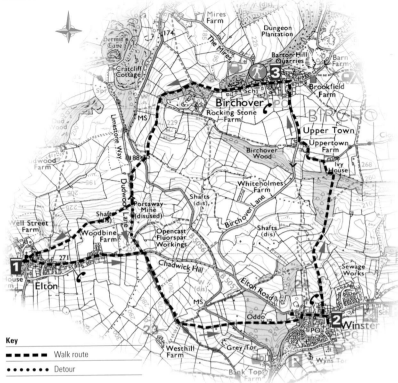

Key

■ ■ ■ ■ Walk route

● ● ● ● ● ● Detour

tinue straight ahead down the no through road (actually still called Main Street) on a track past the Old Vicarage with its well-stocked garden and pond. Ignore paths leading first left and then right, keeping instead to the good wide track that follows the contour around the hill; pass through a gate (via a stile) and then just as you bear left around the corner (with views ahead to Elton and its church) you'll see paths leading off both right and, a few yards later, left. Our route – unsigned – keeps straight ahead. You will pass a barn just before dropping down to cross a tiny stream and then up to meet the road. As you are doing so look across to the right and you'll pick out the weird rock formations of Robin Hood's Stride emerging from the woodland. Cross carefully through the stile opposite and in a few yards you'll meet a much

quieter lane (Dudwood Lane) by some houses.

This byway follows the line of the Portway, one of Derbyshire's ancient trackways, which linked Derby and Chester, and may even pre-date the Romans (see also Walk 1). Head left uphill for a few minutes and look out for a footpath

The gritstone outcrop of Robin Hood's Stride

Fireplace in the simply furnished Duke of York Inn, Elton

sign about 75 yards beyond the roadside barn. Take this path through some very attractive meadows and head straight towards the tower of Elton church, which soon comes into view. The village is set on an interesting geological division: limestone on the north side and an island of gritstone on the south. Botanists will be able to observe this through the different plant species, and the houses are built of both materials in this rather austere settlement. The proximity both to the nearby lead veins and the Portway may have been some compensation for the site of the village, almost a thousand feet high. Right opposite the church stands Elton's only pub, the **Duke of York Inn** 🄁.

Of all pubs in this guide, this is the plainest and simplest of the lot but the welcome is warm and friendly and, once the pub opens, the cosy back room soon fills up with locals, and nothing interrupts the sound of conversation. The old and unspoiled fittings of this three-room public house are a real treasure in this age of transient tastes and frequent makeovers. Mary Elliott, the licensee (who runs the Duke with her nephew), has been associated for 40 years with the pub which until 1968 was in the estate of Offilers, a Derby brewer now long-deceased. Expect your cask ales (Adnams, Black Sheep and Marston's Pedigree) to be in excellent condition. The food, however, is resolutely traditional and minimalist – crisps and peanuts! As there are three separate rooms in the pub, children are welcome.

Across the street is the famous cyclists' café, which is only open on Sundays.

It's a hard pub to leave, but heading for Winster either retrace your steps on the footpath back to the minor lane (Dudwood Lane) and turn right or, if you can't bear to walk the same path twice, take the road down through the village to join Dudwood Lane at a later point further south. Now continue on the Portway southwards (a right turn from the road from Elton) for about 500 yards to a junction where a lane crosses the Portway at approximately 90 degrees. Here you'll find a path going to the left at about 45 degrees. Take this which will lead you quickly to the B5056. Cross carefully onto a good track opposite, which takes you into Winster in a few minutes, via the curious looking parish church and its tranquil graveyard. Emerge at the end of Winster's impressive main street by Dower House.

The contrast in prosperity between Winster's houses and those at Elton is unmistakable. Winster was surrounded by numerous productive lead mines. At the height of the mining boom in the mid-18th century it was the fourth largest town in Derbyshire. Near to the *Miners' Standard* pub, a shanty town of miners' huts sprung up, close to the Portway Mine, one of the richest mines in the county. But the boom only lasted

Attractive houses in Winster village

At the heart of the village the Duke of York Inn, Elton

a century or so until foreign competition and the soaring cost of draining the mines put them out of business. The village retains its pleasant 18th-century character, with more than 60 listed buildings in its Conservation Area. Walk past Winster Hall, an early Georgian house, admiring its impressive central pilasters and top balustrade – this was a pub until about twenty years ago! Just beyond is the Old Market Hall, the National Trust's first Derbyshire acquisition; and just off to the right here is the **Old Bowling Green 2** . This free house is quite upmarket with an emphasis on food but they don't neglect their beers, as evidenced by the good choice of ales. Theakston's Bitter is accompanied by two changing guest beers, and like many Peakland pubs the Bowling Green makes good use of Derbyshire's impressive list of good-quality micros, like Thornbridge and Bradfield. Dogs are

welcome, as are children, the latter until 9pm in the rear dining room. However, don't get caught out by the rather restricted opening hours…the *Miners' Standard* (see 'Try Also') is a nearby alternative if you do: follow the road (East Bank) round steeply uphill until it rejoins the main road above the village.

Leaving the Old Bowling Green, pick up Woodhouse Lane by the shop almost opposite the Market Hall. This path leads steadily down towards the bottom of the deep valley that separates Winster from Birchover. Keep on going and where waymarks indicate a fork in the path at the valley bottom, keep on the right hand option and climb on setts – quite steep near the top – to reach a lane (Clough Lane). Bizarrely you may even have some ostriches for company for the last few yards. There are good views back to Winster as you head left along the winding little lane, and a right turn at the next junction takes you quickly into Birchover's main street, and a minute downhill, the **Red Lion Inn 3** . Under new management, this old pub manages to offer an ambitious menu alongside well-kept beers (Black Sheep Bitter with one or two guest ales). Opened out to an extent, the pub does retain a 'ramblers' bar' which in the evenings becomes a lively village local. Note the old well, visible through a glass plate in the floor. Children are welcome until 9.15pm.

PUB INFORMATION

1 Duke of York Inn
Main Street, Elton
Matlock, Derbyshire DE4 2BW
01629 650367
Hours: 8–11; 12–3, 8.30–10.30 Sun
Food: light snacks only
CAMRA National Inventory

2 Old Bowling Green
East Bank, Winster
Matlock, Derbyshire DE4 2DS
01629 650219
Hours: closed Mon–Tue; 6–11.30;
12–3, 6–10.30 Sun
Food: 6–9 daily

3 Red Lion Inn
Main Street, Birchover
Matlock, Derbyshire DE4 2BN

01629 650363
Hours: 12–2.30 (3 Sun), 7–11
(10.30 Sun)
Food: lunchtimes & evenings

TRY ALSO:

Miners' Standard
Bank Top, Winster
Matlock, Derbyshire DE4 2DR
01629 650279

Local attractions: Robin Hood's Stride; Stanton Moor and Stone Circle (Nine Ladies), 1 mile – see Walk 9; Arbor Low stone circle, 5 miles; Winster Old Market Hall (National Trust); Haddon Hall, 4 miles.

Distinctive pub sign at the Red Lion Inn, Birchover

sheffield group

above: **Hathersage**   below: **Winnats Pass near Castleton**

Bradfield Dale and the Loxley Valley from Sheffield

WALK INFORMATION

Start: Loxley road, by Low Matlock Lane, near Malin Bridge tram stop, Sheffield (◎ 317898)

Finish: Nag's Head, Loxley

Access: Stagecoach Rural Rider 61, 62 from Hillsborough Interchange. Supertram to Hillsborough

Distance: 7½ miles (11 km); 5¼ miles (8.5 km) circuit from the Nag's Head. OS Map: Explorer OL1

The walk: A simple walk, with no major climbs

The pubs: Old Horns Inn, High Bradfield; Plough Inn, Low Bradfield; Nag's Head, Loxley

Despite the proximity to Sheffield, the Loxley Valley has a surprisingly rural feel. A cascade of reservoirs occupies the upper part of the valley, which becomes Bradfield Dale. The area has had a turbulent history, both as an important location for water-powered industry and as the scene of the Great Sheffield Flood of 1864. Happily, a new industry has taken the place of the old: a successful micro-brewery in Bradfield village. Having taken you up Loxley Valley to start, the walk climbs above the valley to take in some great views before dropping to Bradfield and returning along the Dam Flask Reservoir. The walk could be shortened, if desired, by omitting the two-mile Loxley Valley section and carrying on to the Nag's Head pub on the bus. Route-finding is fairly straightforward.

Start on the Loxley Road at Low Matlock Lane bus stop. Buses 61 and 62 stop here, although it's only a short walk from the Malin Bridge supertram stop. An unsigned right of way leads down a wide track on the left by the bus stop which veers right after 100 yards round an old industrial building and then continues up the valley. The route is pretty straightforward: you turn left (down Black Lane) and after about 10 minutes, upon reaching a T-junction, take a

Heather moors covering the hilltops to the west of High Bradfield

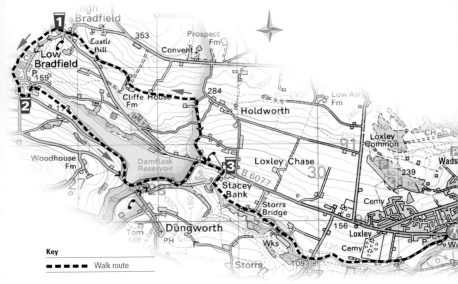

Key

━ ━ ━ ━ Walk route

narrowing path which shortly joins the river, skirts a pond and becomes more shaded. On reaching a road, the path continues ahead about 20 yards down to your left. Carry on in a northwesterly direction, meandering along beside the river (always on your left). All sorts of old mills once occupied this valley which now has its fair share of dereliction, although the controversial Loxley Village development is going through the planning process as this book went to press. Disregard

High Bradfield village street

paths forking off to the left just before a fish pond and carry on until you are just about to reach the foot of the outflow from the reservoir ahead (you'll only see the cascade and a steep bank at this stage!) by a T-junction of paths. Turn right and walk up the lane (Stacey Lane) to emerge on the main Loxley Road a few yards from the Nag's Head (⊙ 288907). The walk finishes here later on so depending upon whether the pub is open, you may or may not wish to visit at this point.

If not visiting the pub, turn left at Loxley Road and after a couple of hundred yards take a pleasant little lane off to the right (Back Lane) which winds about half a mile up the hillside, quite steeply at times. Ignore first a lane off to the right and go straight over a crossroads until, just before a T-junction, you'll spot a footpath (signed to Bradfield) running to the left. Climbing up here enables you to see the geography of the valley: below you the large Dam Flask Reservoir, the lowest of the cascade known as the Bradfield Scheme. This reservoir was built after the Great Sheffield Flood, March 11th, 1864. This was when the Dale Dyke embankment further up the valley burst, around midnight, releasing some 700 million gallons of water. This mass of energy surged down the Loxley Valley towards Malin Bridge, Hillsborough and beyond, sweeping through Owlerton, Neepsend, Kelham Island,

The Watch House, St Nicholas's Church   The attractive St Nicholas's Church, High Bradfield

and even further towards Rotherham. More than 240 people died, making it the worst disaster in England in the 19th century. A memorial plaque to remember the event, and those who lost their lives, was dedicated in Bradfield Parish Church in 1989. There are also wide views across to the moors on the other side of the valley, and to the village of Dungworth.

Keep to the field boundary but watch the stiles, which take you from one side to the other. At Cliff House Farm, a great view opens out before you. Take the wide farm track through and beyond the farm and over a couple of fields but, just before joining Loxley road, look for a footpath off uphill to the right. This leads you into Bradfield via a small escarpment with superb views. At the road simply turn left and walk down into the village, where you will find the **Old Horns Inn** **1**.

The Old Horns Inn, Bradfield

A modernised interior in a traditional stone building, this pub has a smart L-shaped drinking area and a separate, highly-rated restaurant. The Horns is a rare Peak tied house of the Thwaites Brewery, with four handpumps dispensing their beers: Original, Thoroughbred, Bomber and a seasonal guest ale. Children are welcome.

Leaving the pub, follow the village street along to the church. The attractive houses were once home to a domestic knitting industry, but St Nicholas's Church beyond is the architectural star of the show hereabouts. The Grade I listed, 15th-century building looks as if it belongs in a bigger settlement than this. There's also a curious Watch House in the churchyard, built to guard the graveyard from body-snatchers! Follow the path which leads to the left of and around the churchyard and then, after dropping a few yards, resumes in the same direction leading you downhill, parallel to the road on your left with a line of mature trees for company. Lower down you'll catch a glimpse of the Agden Reservoir. Emerge at a lane in trees where the footpath continues across and leads down to a small brook. Cross this and follow the narrow path on its right bank to join the road in Low Bradfield. Here turn left again and it's a short walk up Mill Lee Road to the welcoming **Plough Inn** **2**.

The Plough is currently the real ale destination in the valley thanks to the efforts of Chris and Mandy, the licensees, who moved in last

Agden Reservoir, built in 1869 to collect water off the moorland, seen from High Bradfield

year. They know how to look after their beers having steered their previous pub into the *Good Beer Guide*. They are firm supporters of the local Bradfield brewery – the house beer is brewed by Bradfield – and there's normally at least one other Bradfield beer and a guest ale. The building has been heavily modernised (with a comfortable eating extension at the far end of the long building for busy times) but happily still retains a separate public bar where dogs can join the paying public. Children are welcome and there's a play area and rear beer garden.

Leaving the Plough turn right and after 50 yards a footpath heads left (School Lane) by the old police house straight down to the valley bottom where, before the bridge, an excellent concession path leads off right and follows the banks of the Dam Flask Reservoir all the way. It's an easy as well as an attractive stroll, and a pleasant contrast to the high level route into the village. Eventually, just before the dam itself, the path rejoins the road (New Road) from where it's a short walk across the head of the dam and right to the **Nag's Head** **3**.

This former Kimberley house has a clean and compact interior with separate areas although it has been opened out to some extent. Expect Hardy & Hanson's Bitter and usually something else from the Greene King range. From here the bus service runs during the day back to Sheffield. However, do check the timetable before you set out unless you want to pay for a taxi!

PUB INFORMATION

1 **Old Horns Inn**
High Bradfield
Sheffield S6 6LG
0114 285 1207
Hours: 12-4, 5.30-midnight
Mon-Tue & Thu; 12-midnight Wed,
Fri-Sun
Food: 12-2.30, 5.30-9 (8 Sun)

2 **Plough Inn**
New Road, Low Bradfield
Sheffield S6 6HW
0114 285 1280
Hours: 12-3, 7-11 Mon-
Tue; 12-11 Wed-Sun
Food: 12-2.30 (3 Sun, not
Mon-Tue), 5.30-8.30 (6-8 Sun)

3 **Nag's Head**
Stacey Bank, Loxley
Sheffield S6 6SJ
0114 285 1202
Hours: 12-11.30 daily
Food: Please ring to check times

Local attractions: Sheffield attractions (see www.sheffield.gov.uk);
Yorkshire Sculpture Park, Junction
38 on the M1 (www.ysp.co.uk).

The 300-year-old
Plough Inn, Bradfield

A pleasantly shaded lane near
Bradfield, perfect for walking

Castleton and the Upper Hope Valley

WALK INFORMATION

Start/Finish: Castleton Market Place (150829)

Access: 272 from Sheffield; Hulleys 173 from Bakewell and Tideswell; other local services, see *Peak District Bus Timetable*. Nearest rail station Hope (2 miles) – it's possible to start and finish here instead

Distance: 6½ miles (10.5 km) for round trip (4½ miles to Hope). OS Map: Explorer OL1

The walk: An easy circuit of one of the Peak's most popular valleys

The pubs: Cheshire Cheese, Hope. Option to visit Woodroffe Arms, Hope

View from Mam Tor of the Vale of Hope and the village of Castleton

An easy climb up onto the ridge separating the Hope and Edale valleys from one of the Peak District's busiest visitor honeypots. Excellent views abound, Mam Tor and the Winnats being among the highlights, with the alluring prospect of a visit to the CAMRA Derbyshire Pub of the Year 2007/2008. The paths are good even in mist, so navigation should be straightforward and it's also generally good underfoot with possibility of boggy sections near Mam Tor. The Cheshire Cheese shuts in the afternoon, and to get there for lunch you will need a reasonably early start from Castleton, maybe by 11am. An even earlier start from (and finish at) Hope is recommended.

Start in Castleton market place adjacent to the Castle pub. There are plenty of tea rooms here if you want to take the opportunity to fortify yourselves before setting off. Walk up the village square past the youth hostel and turn right up the narrow lane with the village chip shop on your left. Ahead of you at the top of the square is the entrance to Peveril Castle, which stands guard over the village – you'll get a better

Key

▬ ▬ ▬ ▬ ▬ Walk route

The limestone gorge, the Winnats, seen from Castleton

long ridge, which separates the Hope Valley from the Vale of Edale. This pleasant path drops you back on the road at the foot of the Winnats, right by the Speedwell Cavern, one of several underground show caves for which Castleton is well-known (see information box) – this one has the distinction of being entered in water. There's an excellent view up the pass, (and there's nothing to stop you walking up it for a look) but since the closure of the Mam Tor road the Winnats is once again the only route through at the head of the valley. The road is not overly busy but the traffic does detract a little from the grandeur of the scene. Continue almost straight across by Speedwell and very soon the path will drop you down to the old road just short of another cave, the Treak Cliff Cavern. The road below Mam Tor, which is now closed to traffic, was first built in 1819 by the Sheffield Turnpike Company using spoil from the nearby Odin mine. The route was designed to bypass the steep Winnats Pass,

view of it looking back later in the walk. Carry on to another cluster of older houses around a small stream. Still going in the same direction, the route proceeds uphill past a 'No through road' sign and bears right, becoming a footpath by a gate. The navigation from now on is easy.

Almost immediately you're treated to fine views towards the limestone gorge ahead: this is the Winnats, which at one time carried the main road through the village and westwards. Further right you're looking across to Mam Tor and the

where the one-in-five gradient was a severe test of horses' strength and coachman's skill.

However, Mam Tor is not known as the 'Shivering Mountain' for nothing and, as a result of continual landslips, the road was difficult to keep open, having to be repaired on a regular basis. Finally the County Council admitted to the futility of the task and shut the route to traffic in 1979. Walk up the deserted road, noting the abandoned entrance to the Odin mine on your left, until at the end of the tarmac (A, ⊙, 133842) where a gated path leads down to Mam Farm, take the good path climbing to the left of the trees up on to the hillside. This well-worn route leads fairly gently up on to the ridge at Hollins Cross. The worst problem you're likely to encounter are a couple of very boggy sections where water seeps out of these unstable cliffs. Once on the ridge there are fine views in all directions. North across the Vale of Edale lie the high moors of Kinderscout; back along the ridge lies Mam Tor itself, the abandoned road at its foot. There's also a fine view back across to Castleton where Peveril Castle is now prominent above the village. Less welcome is the cement factory, which you may have already come across on the Hathersage walk!

Walk along the ridge away from Mam Tor – in good weather expect the ridge to be thronged with walkers of all shapes and sizes, and hang gliders taking advantage of the good updraughts. Head to the right on another good path into the trees just before the steep section on the ridge,

The old road, visibly destroyed by landslips, skirting Mam Tor

THE CAVES AND CAVERNS OF THE CASTLETON AREA

Where the geological conditions are favourable, the solubility of limestone in water, over time, often leads to the development of extensive cave systems. Castleton is not the only place in the Peak District with caves but its fame derives from the four show caves here, three of which are not entirely natural, having been widened by mining activity. The exception is the Peak Cavern (also known as the Devil's Arse!) but this is by no means the largest natural cave here. The Titan Cavern nearby, discovered in 1999, is the longest free hanging pitch in any known UK cave, some 464 ft (141 m), linking the Peak Cavern with the nearby Speedwell Cavern.

Much of the mining was due to lead (the nearby Odin mine was probably even worked during Roman occupation) but also because of Blue John, a coloured fluorspar (or fluorite) which is a mineral deposit occurring in veins and associated with metallic deposits as well as limestone. Despite what locals might tell you it is not unique to Castleton although it has been mined here for a long time, and the yellow-blue deposits are very beautiful and have been used in jewellery, vases and other pottery. The name probably derives from the French 'bleu-jaune'.

and on emerging from the woodland follow along the path for another 15 minutes or so (and a few stiles) until, where one path comes down from the left off the hillside, another grass path peels off right down the hillside on this side of the fence

just before another stile. Take this downhill route via a line of oak trees until Crimea Farm is reached — it's invisible until you're almost upon it. Disregard the signpost to 'Hope and Castleton' leading right and instead walk around the top of the farmhouse until at the stile beyond, a footpath to Hope (not 'Hope and Edale' straight ahead) leads you through another stile and then straight downhill on a well signed and pleasant stroll towards the village.

Just before you reach a railway bridge (if you do, you've gone too far, so turn back!) turn left at a crosspath towards Edale, which reaches the Edale road in a couple of minutes. It's now a very short walk to the right, under the rail bridge, and you'll arrive at the **Cheshire Cheese** ⬛1. There's a cheerful welcome to walkers outside, and indeed this is no ordinary pub since it was awarded Derbyshire Pub of the year by CAMRA for 2007/2008. By the time you visit, however, there will be new management — as we go to press the pub has been bought by Enterprise Inns. Hopefully they will continue to maintain the excellent range of well-kept beers dispensed from five handpumps on the bar, the obliging

The Cheshire Cheese, dating back to the 16th century

service and the well-regarded food. There's a separate room primarily for diners on a lower level, which allows the rest of the place to retain a pubby atmosphere in which to enjoy your beer. The whole pub although slightly opened out still retains a great deal of character.

It's a walk of a few minutes down the road to the right when you come out of the Cheshire Cheese to the village centre on the main road. Here there are two more pubs offering a range of real ales. The improved *Woodroffe Arms* in particular may be worth a visit before heading back to Castleton. There are infrequent buses but the path back across the meadows (just under 2 miles) is easy and pleasant. Take the lane on the right by the parish church. Follow it down to the river bridge and start up the hill on the other side before picking up a signed footpath, which you then follow all the way. This eventually brings you to the main road just east of Castleton Village, and from here it's simply a five-minute walk past the souvenir shops and guesthouses back to the walk's starting point.

PUB INFORMATION

⬛1 **Cheshire Cheese**
Edale Road, Hope
Derbyshire S33 6ZF
01433 620381
Hours: 12–3, 6–11; 12–11 Sat; 12–10.30 Sun
Food: lunchtimes and evenings

TRY ALSO:

Woodroffe Arms
1 Castleton Road, Hope
Derbyshire S33 6SB
01433 620351

Local attractions: Peveril Castle ruins; Castleton Museum, Buxton Road; Winnats (natural gorge), ½ mile; Castleton show caves and Bagshawe Cavern, Bradfield, 3 miles.

A welcome sight outside the Cheshire Cheese

HIKERS
THIS HOSTELRY IS RENOWNED
AS A HIKERS RESTING PLACE
WE DO NOT REQUIRE THE
REMOVAL OF BOOTS & PACKS
USE THE BOOT SCRAPER AND
FEEL FREE TO ENTER

CAR OWNERS
PLEASE PARK SENSIBLY
ON ONE SIDE ONLY AND DO NOT
OBSTRUCT ANY ENTRANCES

FREE HOUSE

Hathersage Circuit via Padley Gorge and Carl Wark

WALK INFORMATION

Start/Finish: Grindleford rail station (◉, 250788)

Access: Limited rail services from Sheffield and Manchester. Buses 65, 215 from Sheffield / Buxton / Wirksworth; 240 from Bakewell, all stop at Mount Pleasant close by

Distance: 7 miles (11 km) for round trip (4½ miles to Hathersage). OS Map: Explorer OL1, OL24

The walk: A popular circular route. Challenging in poor visiblity

The pubs: Little John Hotel, Millstone Country Inn, both Hathersage

In 1893 Totley Tunnel, Britain's second longest rail tunnel, brought the railway from Sheffield to the relatively isolated Hope Valley. Grindleford was the first stop and the area prospered as a result. Padley Gorge became a top walkers' destination, a place it continues to hold within the Peak District. There's a car park adjacent to the station and a café which has assumed near legendary status among the Sheffield walking fraternity. You may wish to try it out before setting off. This is a deservedly popular walk with a good variety of scenery taking in both Padley Gorge and the open moorland west of Sheffield, before finishing with a delightful riverside stroll back to the station café. Unless you're confident in hill navigation it's probably one to avoid in mist unless you simply stick to the low-level route along the river. In clear conditions, the navigation is straightforward and the terrain moderate.

Start at Grindleford rail station and head north over the railway bridge and, disregarding the sign to the Longshaw estate, pass through a stile to the right after about 50 yards into National Trust land signed 'Padley Gorge'. Follow the track up through the wooded gorge,

View of Higger Tor, looking towards Hope Valley and the cement works

with the river never far away, babbling on your left. Either take the footbridge that you'll see in a couple of hundred yards and walk up the other side of the stream or simply stay on the path you're already on – either way the navigation is simple: follow the stream for about a mile

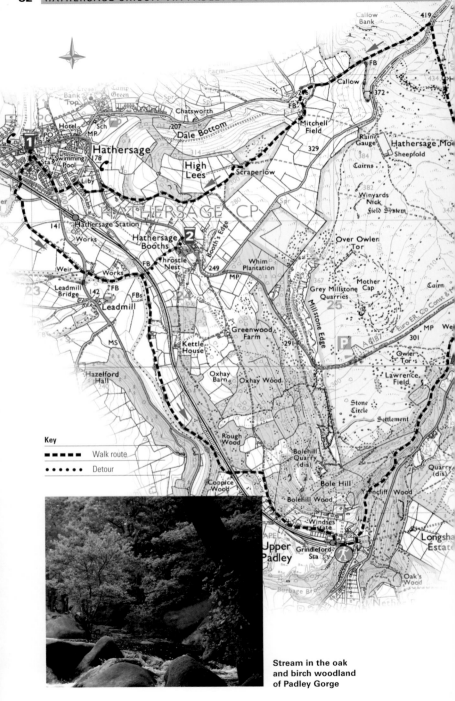

Key

━ ━ ━ Walk route

• • • • • Detour

Stream in the oak
and birch woodland
of Padley Gorge

until it emerges out of the trees at a spot close to the main Sheffield to Hathersage road (A, 257800). In good weather this is a popular picnic spot. Cross the stream by the footbridge a hundred yards further up (unless you did so lower down) and continue up, keeping the stream on your right now to a second footbridge (where a stone sett path leads up beyond) – don't cross at this bridge, however, but stay on the left-hand side of the river until you reach the road by a stile in another hundred yards. Now you'll see two signs – disregard the one immediately opposite and walk carefully right along the roadside for 50 yards (and cross with care) to the opposite side where, on the bend, a second footpath is signed onto the open moor. Go up onto the small ridge rather than following the stream, and pick up a path through the heather towards two rocky outcrops ahead of you.

The nearer one is Carl Wark, an escarpment hill fort, probably fortified in the Iron Age; it uses natural sheer cliffs on three sides to provide an easily defended position. Your track to Higger Tor beyond skirts the left edge of it so you can easily divert and walk around the ramparts. The view from Higger Tor is even wider, especially westwards to the Hope Valley where the remarkably ugly cement factory unfortunately dominates the vista and offsets the natural beauty. Carry on over Higger Tor to a good track down to the big car park but after 50 yards or so turn left down a track towards the road at the nearest point to you – you should be able to see a footpath sign down at the roadside. Go straight across the road onto another track and turn left after about 20 yards down a steep path that winds through the heather (and may be muddy in places) past a ruin, and down to a bridge over a stream (B, 249819) where you turn left to Mitchell Field Farm. Ignore footpath signs off this track until, beyond the farm buildings, a sign directs you to the right into the trees and across another stile. Then the path is clear leading across to, through and beyond a large house (Scraperlow on the map) with incongruously manicured lawns. The track then runs pleasantly through open woodland with good views to the

The Little John Hotel, Hathersage

Derwent Valley below and becomes wider leading you down to the A6187 road on the outskirts of Hathersage.

It's not a lot of fun to walk down the main road into town so turn left for 50 yards crossing the road and take the signed path by the bus stop down to a lane where left again to the bottom and right along the B6001 leads you into the village centre right by the first pub. The **Little John Hotel** **1** is a rambling building with a few interesting interwar features including some surviving stained glass. This free house has developed a reputation for serving a wide range of interesting guest beers together with generous portions of tempting food. Although opened out internally there are several distinct areas inside. You might also want to visit the alleged grave of Little John, Robin Hood's faithful companion, in the churchyard nearby, before carrying on walking.

Hathersage today is an upmarket sort of place, unlike the 19th-century version when it had several dirty mills manufacturing buttons, needles and wire, as well as turning out millstones. Your best bet for another pub is the **Millstone Country Inn** **2**, about a mile east (uphill on the main road). To get there avoiding the dismal roadside walk, there's an hourly bus (route 272 in the *Peak District Bus Timetable*), or a short climb from further along

Original Victorian street furniture at Hathersage **Shady path near Scraperlow**

the walk (see * below). The Millstone is quite an upmarket, food-oriented affair but it serves up to three local guest beers (there are tasting notes that should help you choose correctly) alongside Taylor Landlord and Black Sheep Bitter. It has a popular 'pick and mix' sausage and mash selection alongside the wide-ranging main menu.

The views from the front windows vie for the accolade of the finest views you can enjoy whilst indoors on Peak District licensed premises.

It's possible to take the train back to Sheffield or Manchester from Hathersage station but I'd strongly recommend the riverside walk back to Grindleford. From the Little John, take the charming little minor road which drops down the right hand side of the pub as you look at the frontage, and where the road bends round sharply to the left, look for a footpath signed to Leadmill Bridge. This leads across the meadows to the main road where you go straight across to pick up a riverside path. This follows the river sharp right after about 300 yards (* at this point the path, branching left under the railway bridge, takes you steeply but quickly up to the Millstone Country Inn) and quickly assumes a pleasant rural character leading you under wooded bluffs and alongside grassy meadows. Eventually you'll see a path, diverging left, signed to Grindleford Station. Climb up through the woods and across the railway bridge where, heading uphill for another 50 yards or so, you'll see a clear track to the right which leads you unerringly back towards the station via Padley Chapel. This forlorn gatehouse-chapel is all that remains of Padley Hall, a large medieval manor house built in the 14th century (open Wednesday and Sunday afternoons from 2pm).

huddersfield group

top: **Boats entering the Standedge Tunnel** bottom: **Millstones on the moor**

Over Standedge to Marsden from Greenfield or Diggle

WALK INFORMATION

Start: Greenfield station or Diggle; by the entrance to Standedge Tunnel

Finish: Riverhead Brewery Tap, Marsden

Access: Rail from Huddersfield or Manchester, or route 184 (First Bus), from Huddersfield-Oldham-Manchester, hourly. Other buses from Marsden to Huddersfield

Distance: 4 miles (6.5 km) from Diggle. OS Maps: Explorer OL1, OL24

The walk: A hilltop walk with extensive views. More challenging in poor visibility

The pubs: Tunnel End Inn, Riverhead Brewery Tap, both Marsden. Option to visit Sair Inn, Linthwaite

Standedge Visitor Centre, once a canal warehouse

This walk follows a section of canal towpath followed by an exhilarating traverse of the Pennine watershed above Standedge Tunnel with extensive views. You finish in a typical Pennine mill town in a splendid setting. Marsden is now becoming a genuine beer destination with two reliable pubs offering a wide range of beers; and both offer food where your children can join you. The route crosses high and exposed moorland, although the tracks are clear and navigation is straightforward, even in mist. Nonetheless you should be a confident hill walker and suitably clothed to attempt the route in poor weather, when you might consider using a bus over the summit section and simply turn it into a towpath walk that could be extended towards Huddersfield.

Starting from Greenfield (extra 3 miles/5 km): the Huddersfield narrow canal, although closed and segmented for many years was re-opened by HRH Prince of Wales on 3rd September 2001, and is now part of the increasingly popular South Pennine Ring waterway route.

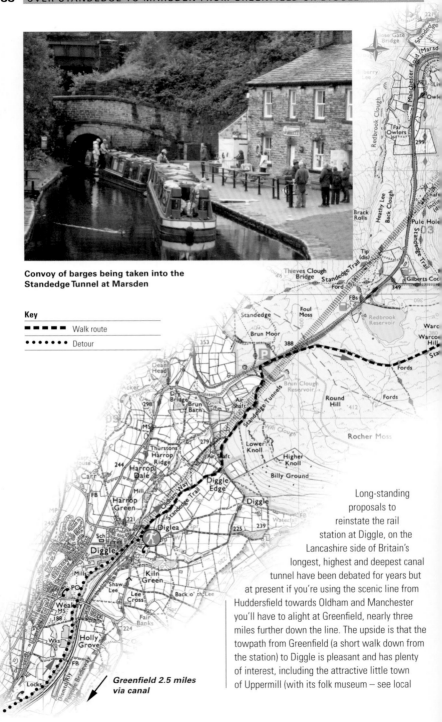

Convoy of barges being taken into the Standedge Tunnel at Marsden

Key
■ ■ ■ ■ ■ Walk route
● ● ● ● ● ● Detour

Long-standing proposals to reinstate the rail station at Diggle, on the Lancashire side of Britain's longest, highest and deepest canal tunnel have been debated for years but at present if you're using the scenic line from Huddersfield towards Oldham and Manchester you'll have to alight at Greenfield, nearly three miles further down the line. The upside is that the towpath from Greenfield (a short walk down from the station) to Diggle is pleasant and has plenty of interest, including the attractive little town of Uppermill (with its folk museum – see local

Greenfield 2.5 miles via canal

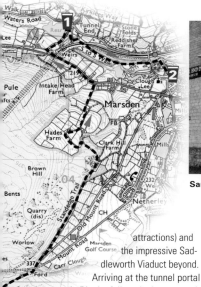

Sandstone exterior of the Tunnel End Inn, Marsden

attractions) and the impressive Saddleworth Viaduct beyond. Arriving at the tunnel portal in Diggle, follow the lane up and over the railway line to the Diggle Hotel, an attractive building worth patronising if you find yourself trying the route in reverse. From the rail bridge, three railway tunnels can be seen: the original (1849) single-track one is in the centre with the 1871 tunnel on the right. Both of these are disused, superseded by the twin-track bore built in 1894.

Take the gravel track (Boat Lane) on the left-hand side of the hotel (part of the new Pennine Bridleway). The railway lies in a deep cutting to your left as it approaches the tunnel. Follow the track up the hill with good views opening up behind you. When you reach the tarmac by a row of cottages and the road bears left, head off at 45 degrees to the right almost immediately on the signed Pennine Bridleway/Oldham Way. Meander around spoil heaps from the tunnel construction to bear left at a derelict cottage. In front and above is a dam with a gateway at the left-hand end. Head for this gate, leaving the Pennine Bridleway here and following the signed path 'Standedge car park'. On the track adjacent to the main road, skirt the little Brun Clough Reservoir, built to service the canal and 600 ft directly above the tunnel. Just ahead, after the car park, you join the Pennine Way as it climbs up on the side of Standedge Cutting, running parallel to the A62 before veering right through a gate onto a wide grass track. This was once the turnpike road over the Pennine watershed. It contours around the Redbrook Reservoir and towards the conical Pule Hill, while the Pennine Way veers away southwards. If the weather's good, pause to enjoy the wide views here especially westwards. In poor weather this is a very exposed location, although you're never very far from civilisation.

You'll see a quiet road (Mount Road) ahead as you near the eastern flank of Pule Hill. A wooden post marks where the turnpike has been washed away by a stream but follow the track beyond here to drop down to a plank bridge and to the tarmac at the point where it bifurcates and Old Mount Road diverges left. A few yards up here an unsurfaced lane bears left off this, signposted to Hades Farm

Excellent view over the old mill town of Marsden

and Standedge Trail. Fine views start to open up of Butterley Reservoir and, when you get higher up, over Marsden and down the Colne Valley towards Huddersfield. The track soon swings left over a rise and drops down to Hades Farm, where you go through the gate stile and turn right down to New Hey Farm below it. The only bit of navigation which requires care is here, where the desired right of way goes straight downhill (not the signed path veering right) to another wooden stile and then down through a very narrow section between hedge and fence to emerge on the A62 at the right-hand end of the terrace of cottages below you. Cross here and turn left, walking alongside the road for about 400 yards before dropping right, down the first minor road (Ainsley Lane). Here there is an excellent view over Tunnel End where the relationship of the three railway tunnels with the canal tunnel is clearly visible. Follow the lane round to the right and directly to a very welcome sight, the excellent **Tunnel End Inn** 🔢 (🔘 040121).

The Tunnel End Inn is enthusiastically run by Gary and Bev Earnshaw who have turned the favourably sited pub into a real ale destination, a stone's throw from the Standedge Visitor Centre at the tunnel mouth. Home-cooked food complements the four hand-pulled ales (including a changing guest beer) from the likes of Timothy Taylor and Black Sheep. The pub offers self-

The welcoming bar of the Riverhead Brewery Tap, and its large selection of fine ales.

catering accommodation for up to four people in a town rather short of visitor beds; and they offer free soft drinks for designated drivers and go as far as opening the pub outside regular hours for groups – ring ahead to check.

From the Tunnel End it's a simple 10-minute walk into town: take the lane opposite straight down to the canal and visitor centre (about a minute's walk). Now follow the towpath and you'll arrive at Marsden station, where you simply head down Station Road to reach the **Riverhead Brewery Tap** 🔢 in a couple of minutes. Sited right by the bridge at the foot of the main street, the Tap and its brewhouse are enjoying a new lease of life as part of the small estate of the Ossett brewery, who are not only making a very a good job of producing the Riverhead beers, named after local reservoirs, but also offer a wide range of their own excellent ales in addition. The ambience, in a tastefully modernised old corner building with high windows, is agreeable, and with buses and trains close by you can take your time.

If you're feeling energetic there is also a well-known brewpub the *Sair Inn*, a few miles down the canal towards Huddersfield, which offers up to ten ales (🔘 100143).

PUB INFORMATION

🔢 **Tunnel End Inn**
Waters Road, Marsden
Huddersfield, West Yorkshire
HD7 6NF
01484 844636
www.tunnelendinn.com
Hours: 8 (5 Tue-Thu)-11; 12-3,
5-11 Fri; 12-11 Sat; 12-10.30 Sun
Food: 6-9 Wed; 12-2.30 (3 Sat),
6-8 Fri & Sat; 12-4 Sun

🔢 **Riverhead Brewery Tap**
2 Peel Street, Marsden
Huddersfield, West Yorkshire
HD7 6BR
01484 841270
Hours: 12-midnight (1am Fri
& Sat)
Food: lunchtimes and evenings
(in upstairs dining room only)

TRY ALSO:

Sair Inn
Lane Top, Linthwaite,
Huddersfield, West Yorkshire
HD7 5SG
01484 842370

Local attractions: Standedge
Visitor Centre, Tunnel End, Marsden
(www.standedge.co.uk); Saddleworth
Museum and Art gallery, Uppermill
(www.saddleworthmuseum.co.uk).

The Tunnel End Inn
offers fine ales

A Beer Circuit in 'Last of the Summer Wine' Country

WALK INFORMATION

Start/Finish: Holmfirth – by the bus station

Access: Frequent buses from Huddersfield bus station, about 30 minutes away

Distance: 4½ miles (7 km). OS Map: Explorer OL1

The walk: This circuit around the edge of Holmfirth is quite straightforward and fairly short

The pubs: Rose & Crown Inn (or Nook); Hervey's Wine Bar; Old Bridge Inn, all Holmfirth. Option to visit Farmers Arms, Holmfirth

Although better known today for its links with the sitcom *Last of the Summer Wine*, Holmfirth has a long history as a textile centre with a tradition of producing some of the world's finest woollen yarns and cloths. Today, local firms still supply materials to some of the top names in the fashion world. This circular walk offers a flavour not only of the town with its distinctive Pennine mill town architecture but of the rural setting with walled fields intersected by old packhorse trails, while the surrounding moors are never far away. There are a couple of steep pulls but it's only a moderate walk with few navigational problems.

Start the walk at the bus station right in the centre of the old Pennine textile town of Holmfirth (⊙ 143082). You'll notice two of the pubs recommended for later on, the Old Bridge Inn and Hervey's Wine Bar, right by you across the small stream. Follow the road back across the river and bear right at the first junction arriving after a few yards at

Mill workers' houses jostle for space in Holmfirth

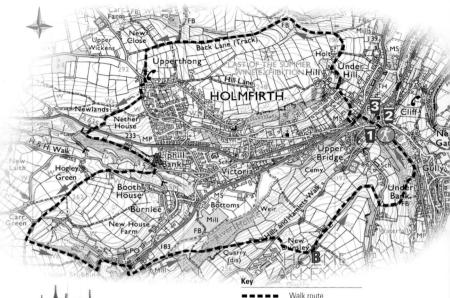

Key

■■■■■ Walk route

Austere church architecture at Holmfirth

the T-junction with the A6024 (Victoria Street/ Huddersfield Road). Here, just across the road to your left, you'll see the Tourist Information Office which you might like to visit before heading up the path immediately beyond it on the right which leads through some gardens (bear right in about 50 yards) to join a minor road. Head left up to the junction of Binns Lane and Holt Lane. Disregard the precipitously steep footpath by No. 1 Holt Lane (although if you want to take it out of interest simply turn right at the top and rejoin the route) and head up Holt Lane on the right, keeping right when the road becomes a trackway.

The settlement of Holmfirth has quickly disappeared and you have about a mile of problem-free navigation as you follow this trackway curving into some charming countryside.

There is a distant view of the Victoria Tower in Huddersfield: the tower, almost 1,000-ft high, was completed in 1899 to celebrate the 60th anniversary of Queen Victoria's reign. Thereafter the track curves around briefly joining a stream but not crossing it and then steadily climbing with rural views. Ignore the first stile on the left but, soon after, the lane merges with a concrete track coming in from your right. Take the next footpath left (good stile, clear path) to quickly emerge in Upperthong by Midgley Farm.

Head downhill on the road (Dean Road) and follow it round to the right (Broad Lane) to take the second of two paths that appear on the right in quick succession. Views change again here: you're looking at the moorlands of the Dark Peak around Holme Moss, and you should be able to see the A6024 road snaking up to the summit. Follow the good path down to the main road (A635) and straight across; and after 100 yards bear left (FP sign) to follow the good track down into a charming wooded valley with a stream running below. Emerge by some houses on a sharp corner at Liphill Bank (A, ⊚, 128078). (If you want to visit the *Farmers Arms* – see 'Try Also' below – follow the lane left here for a few minutes, returning after your visit to this point.)

Go down Liphill Bank Road and turn sharp right into Bank Lane and just after the bridge take the footpath on the right uphill again. Don't get drawn too far to the right, aim instead towards a white cottage with a footpath sign above you visible in a few minutes. The path continues as a track immediately right of this white cottage to Lower Hogley and just beyond, Hogley House. Carry on straight ahead here down to join a lane and head 50 yards up to what turns out to be an old schoolhouse (look for the date of 1816 on the building). A signed footpath curves around behind the house's far hedge and in 150 yards, at the foot of a slope, a clear but unsigned track leads down a very nice dry valley where a steep drop opens out below

you on the left. You should be able to pick out a mill pond and the old mill through the trees.

As you emerge in the small hamlet of Upper Stubbing, the right of way becomes confusing: head to the right by the buildings and immediately before the white house take a narrow track left, becoming well-defined on stone setts. By a second gate, a black swing-gate leads to the left into a seductively dank little dell on a good path to emerge on a minor lane, from where it's 250 yards downhill on Yew Tree Lane to join the main road. Here, take the footpath (signed Hinchliffe Mill) opposite. Go left after a further 50 yards past a fetching old rural industrial terrace of houses and cross the river on a footbridge beyond the mill, following the river downstream for a short way. Then, as you emerge over a broken stile into open meadows with the chimney of

Holmfirth countryside opening out to the moors at the edge of town

Bottoms Mill ahead, take the rising path about 45 degrees right up into some woodland where the track winds uphill over another stile towards the horizon. You'll skirt the face of a disused quarry: look for a junction of paths in the trees where steps join from the left and here go right up a short rise and leave the wood through a gate heading up to the hamlet of houses above you.

From here a concrete driveway leads you up to a minor public road (Brow Lane) with marvellous views over the Holme Valley towards Holmfirth. Almost opposite, take the signed path over a stile with more uphill walking required – it even gets quite steep towards the moor. Look for a blue gate by a small ruin about 500 yards above and make for that. Join the stony lane here (B, , 138073) and follow it left down Ward Bank Road for a few hundred yards or so before it sweeps round to the right in a gentle curve to drop down to another public road (Cartworth Road). Below you lies yet another valley, this time that of the Ribble (no relation to the larger Lancashire twin). Directly opposite, an unsigned path heads quite steeply on a good track down to the valley bottom and then out to the B-road (Dunford Road) no more than five minutes' walk from the centre of Holmfirth.

As you reach the town centre close to your starting spot, look out for a small alleyway leading to Holmfirth's most sequestered pub, the Nook or, more properly, the **Rose & Crown Inn** **1**. If you can't find it, ask a local. There's a

The confusingly signed Rose & Crown Inn

good range of beers served from no fewer than ten handpumps in this atmospheric multi-room and TARDIS-like old pub, which has the distinction of having appeared in every edition of the *Good Beer Guide* since 1976! There's even a rear patio garden. Food is served all day with a separate childrens' menu. Coming out from the pub you'll recognise the bus station across and to your right once you rejoin the main road. Across the little stream from here is the gable end of **Hervey's Wine Bar** **2**, a smart little establishment which keeps good quality real ales in addition to its wine list. Beers from the Skipton micro-brewery, Copper Dragon, are a regular feature alongside a third guest ale. Bar snacks are available lunchtimes and evenings. The **Old Bridge Hotel** **3**, almost alongside, is also worth a look: it's open all day every day and features up to seven real ales including two changing guest beers. Bateman's XB is a regular here alongside Yorkshire beers like Black Sheep and Taylor Landlord. Food is available until 9pm each day; and if you're walking with children The Old Bridge is probably a better bet than Hervey's.

PUB INFORMATION

1 **Rose & Crown Inn**
(The Nook)
7 Victoria Square, Holmfirth
West Yorkshire HD9 2DN
01484 683960
www.thenookpublichouse.co.uk
Hours: 11-11; 12-10.30 Sun
Food: 12-9 Daily

2 **Hervey's Wine Bar**
Norridge Bottom, Holmfirth
West Yorkshire HD9 7BB
01484 686925
www.herveys.co.uk
Hours: closed Mon; 12-midnight summer; 4-midnight winter; 2-midnight Sat & Sun
Food: bar snacks 12-3, 6-9.30 (not Mon)

3 **Old Bridge Hotel**
Market Walk, Holmfirth
West Yorkshire HD9 7DA
01484 681212
www.oldbridgehotel.com
Hours: 12-11 daily

TRY ALSO:

Farmers Arms
Liphill Bank Road, Holmfirth
West Yorkshire, HD9 2LR
01484 683713

Local attractions: 'Last of the Summer Wine' country (see www.summer-wine.com); local art galleries (see www.kirklees.gov.uk/visitorportal), Huddersfield, 5 miles.

buxton group

above: **The Crescent, Buxton** below: **Stone bridge over the Goyt near Strines**

Three Counties and Britain's Highest Village

WALK INFORMATION

Start/Finish: Traveller's Rest, Flash Bar (033677)

Access: Limited public transport. Bus service 118 from Buxton-Hanley-Leek or possibly use the demand-response service from Ashbourne and Leek (see *Peak District Bus Timetable*)

Distance: 5 miles (8 km). OS Map: Explorer OL24

The walk: A straightforward circuit, but it is exposed in parts to the weather – take due care and be prepared

The pubs: New Inn, Flash; Travellers Rest, Flash Bar

A short circular walk taking in a relatively remote and elevated part of the Peak Park, and visiting the highest village in Britain at over 1,500 ft. The village received its official recognition from the Guinness World Records after competition from Wanlockhead in Scotland. It goes without saying that in unpleasant weather some parts are exposed: ensure you are well equipped whatever the weather at the start. Some fine gritstone scenery in the upper reaches of the River Dane, extensive views and two good pubs make this a walk to remember. Watch for closure/limited hours on Mondays and Tuesdays.

Start from the Traveller's Rest at Flash Bar (on the A53), an old toll point on the Leek to Buxton road (although you could quite easily start the walk in the village by the New Inn, half a mile south). Walk carefully up the footpath alongside the main road and cross to the bus shelter and then left up the lane signed 'Knotbury'. Turn right at the first junction after 500 yards, past a collection of rusting cars and where the road bears right to rejoin the A53 go left uphill towards a tiny hamlet. There are wide views as you would expect at an altitude of over 1,500 ft, particularly east to the upper Dove Valley running away to your right and

Expansive view over the Staffordshire moorlands

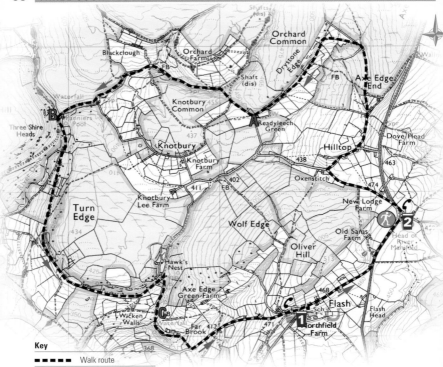

Key
■ ■ ■ ■ ■ Walk route

the moors around Shutlingsloe prominent in the other direction. You can also pick out one of the huge quarries that almost encircle Buxton, more or less ahead of you – at this distance they don't look too disagreeable!

A footpath sign then leads you into Derbyshire through a gate just beyond a rough track

Packhorse trails winding through the hills near Three Shire Heads

on the left and just before the houses. This soon joins a good track with views opening up into the valley beyond. Follow this track round towards a farm where a waymark leads you to the left, just before reaching it. We're back in Staffordshire already! Follow this path easily down to another, lower house where the path becomes a wider vehicle track and runs past a couple of buildings under Drystone Edge joining a quiet lane (A, 🔘 023686). There's a real sense of remoteness in these western moors and you'll probably have the place to yourself as you turn right and climb over the brow of the gentle hill after about 250 yards where a track bears left down to join another lane below. Follow this downhill (bearing left) into a lovely valley to a hollow with Back Clough Farm above you and a footpath sign pointing left. Between these two take the rough track alongside the stream and keep downhill all the way, disregarding other paths, until you reach the infant River Dane by an attractive packhorse bridge at Three Shire Heads (B, 🔘 009685). This peaceful spot was once the site

Restored dining room at the New Inn, Flash

of many illegal prizefights – supposedly because it was easy to escape the law by simply nipping into another county. Today, this is a pleasant and, even in poor weather, relatively sheltered place to pause and, if you have brought them along, open your flask and sandwiches. Old packhorse routes converge here and the Panniers Pool just below the bridge is named after the satchels in which the horses carried their goods. Spring is the best season for birdlife here: dippers, common sandpipers and wagtails feature among the river birds, whilst on the surrounding moors look out for the area's speciality, the ring ouzel, along with lapwings and plovers.

At the bridge you're going to move off left (downstream) but to bag your third county of the day, you could amble across the bridge into

The Upper Dane Valley, an important habitat for birdlife, especially the ring ouzel

Cheshire before crossing back to carry on. The path downstream is good but in places boulder strewn and it forks left onto a higher path at a gate after a few minutes. The views here are excellent with the Dane Valley running away from you towards Gradbach and the Roaches. The path contours around Turn Edge – stay on the path beyond some houses and ignore a wide track doubling back sharply to the right beyond them, but 250 yards further look out for a signed bridleway disappearing sharply back into the trees on your right. This takes you into what feels like a lost valley. Find and cross the footbridge over the stream at the bottom on your left (C, ⊚ 016672) but do not climb the steep path ahead signed 'Flash'. Instead turn sharp right over the bridge, literally on the water's edge, to pick up what becomes a good bridleway bringing you out to the houses at Far Brook, and up a punishingly steep driveway to join a quiet little lane to the village. Turning left here, it's now nearly a half-mile slog steeply uphill on the tarmac but there's little traffic and stupendous views across the Staffordshire moorlands behind you.

As you approach Flash, a sign proclaims it as Britain's highest village (1,518 ft), and it feels like it. The name derives from the term for a swamp, rather than the oft-claimed connections with counterfeiting, although at least one

Bridge, Three Shire Heads – low walls allowed the panniers to be left on the horses

coining machine has been found nearby. When Sir George Crewe, 8th Baronet of Calke Abbey, first visited the parish of Quarnford here in 1819 or 1820, it appeared to him as 'the very end of the civilized world', and Flash itself was 'dirty, and bore marks principally of poverty, sloth, and ignorance'. Things have improved since and the **New Inn** ❶ offers a welcome to all. The pub has been tastefully refurbished to retain a traditional stone floor in the bar area and leading off it, a small but attractive dining area with great views of the Roaches. This child- and dog-friendly village local offers Greene King IPA as a regular along with a guest beer – often from the local Macclesfield Storm brewery. The pub won a local CAMRA branch seasonal award in 2007.

To return to the Traveller's Rest, simply walk up the lane past the primary school and down to the junction with the busy A53. If you want to avoid this short stretch of road, keeping the Traveller's Rest visible to your left, there is a right of way almost opposite the junction which cuts 400 yards across to a minor road where you bear left. Either way you'll soon arrive at the **Traveller's Rest** ❷. One of a number of well-known loftily-sited hostelries offering succour to past travellers across the exposed Pennines, this is a pub I remember reaching on foot in deep snow more than once, whilst snow ploughs wrestled with drifts blowing across the main road off Axe Edge to the north. Whatever the weather, the interior feels welcoming, with several cosy corners leading off the main stone-floored servery. There are all sorts of collectibles to keep the eyes occupied, while the palate is entertained with up to four beers, including the excellent Whim Hartington IPA, Marston's Pedigree and Tetley Bitter (with a summer changing guest ale). If you haven't already eaten in the New Inn, there's an extensive menu here and a dining room down one end of the pub where children can join you.

PUB INFORMATION

❶ **New Inn**
Flash, Quarnford
Buxton, Derbyshire SK17 0SW
01298 22941
Hours: closed Tue; 12 (6 Mon)-midnight
Food: 12-3 (not Mon), 6-9; 12-6 Sun

❷ **Traveller's Rest**
Flash Bar, Quarnford
Buxton, Derbyshire SK17 0SN
01298 23695
Hours: closed Mon; 12-3, 7-11 Tue-Fri; 12-11 Sat & Sun
Food: 12-2.30, 7-9 daily

Local attractions: Buxton Spa, 5 miles; The Roaches (ridge walks and rock climbs), 4 miles; Tittesworth Reservoir and Visitor Centre, 6 miles.

Exterior of the New Inn, Flash

Up the Goyt Valley to Whaley Bridge via New Mills

WALK INFORMATION

Start: Marple at the top of lock flight on the Macclesfield canal (🔍 961887)

Access: Rail to Marple (not Rose Hill); frequent buses from Stockport. Useful early service from Chesterfield via Tideswell – TM Travel local bus service 67. Also buses from Padfield and Glossop. Return buses and trains from Whaley Bridge

Distance: 10 miles (16 km)

The walk: A longer walk with a little bit of everything – sights, nature and, of course, good beer

The pubs: The Sportsman, Strines; Fox Inn, Brookbottom; Dog & Partridge, Bridgemont; Navigation, Buxworth; Shepherd's Inn, Navigation, both Whaley Bridge

The Millennium Walkway, New Mills

An easy linear walk, primarily on canal towpaths, with no navigational difficulties and several excellent pubs along the way that open all day. You can even have a lie-in as the first pub doesn't open until noon! A leisurely start, at say 11am from Marple would be ideal for an all-day saunter. There's a lot of interest along the way particularly in New Mills with the award-winning Millennium Walkway and other attractions, and the historic Bugsworth Canal Basin.

Start at the top of the Marple staircase of locks (a short, steep walk up from the station) and then head south for 400 yards to the top lock on the B6101 (Strines Road). It's a short walk east from the town centre. Canal towpaths are idyllic walking routes, best enjoyed at the slow pace they encourage! Canals diverge after 300 yards: follow the path along the Peak Forest Canal that forks left (the Goyt Way runs along here too for a short distance). Note the handsome little roving bridge (Bridge 19) so-called because its distinctive structure enabled horses to switch sides of the canal. Just over half a mile later, at Pluckbridge, Bridge 21, leave the canal via some steep steps to join a quiet lane and reach the main road in about five minutes. **The Sportsman** 1 is visible some 200 yards to your right down the road. This smart two-bar free house has a strong emphasis on food but with five handpumps dispensing Cains,

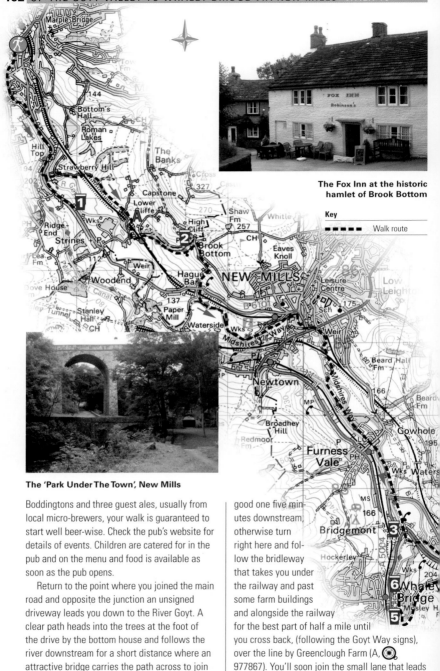

The Fox Inn at the historic hamlet of Brook Bottom

Key

▬ ▬ ▬ ▬ Walk route

The 'Park Under The Town', New Mills

Boddingtons and three guest ales, usually from local micro-brewers, your walk is guaranteed to start well beer-wise. Check the pub's website for details of events. Children are catered for in the pub and on the menu and food is available as soon as the pub opens.

Return to the point where you joined the main road and opposite the junction an unsigned driveway leads you down to the River Goyt. A clear path heads into the trees at the foot of the drive by the bottom house and follows the river downstream for a short distance where an attractive bridge carries the path across to join the Goyt Way. If you're a viaduct junkie there's a good one five minutes downstream, otherwise turn right here and follow the bridleway that takes you under the railway and past some farm buildings and alongside the railway for the best part of half a mile until you cross back, (following the Goyt Way signs), over the line by Greenclough Farm (A, ◉, 977867). You'll soon join the small lane that leads left up to the railway station at Strines; take the tunnel back under the line and then follow the old packhorse road up a good track to emerge in the quiet hamlet of Brook Bottom. This must have once been an important staging post on the ancient route you've just travelled. Fortunately the **Fox Inn** 2 is still very much in business. The pub is comfortable and has a multi-room interior where clearly, former private accommodation has been absorbed into the pub. The Fox is a Robinson's tied house dispensing Best Bitter, Hatter's Mild and a seasonal beer. Lunchtime food finishes at 2pm on weekdays, 6pm at weekends.

From the Fox turn right up the lane climbing until just beyond a seat with views across the Goyt to Disley and beyond; take the signed Goyt Way leading back downhill on the right. The scenery on this stretch is ample recompense for the steep climb up to Brook Bottom. The track goes very steeply downhill through the hamlet of Hague Fold and the old Toll Bar cottage. Cross Hague Bar Road (runs from New Mills to Marple) into Waterside Road and then almost immediately over the railway bridge bear left into Torrs Riverside Park. Follow the narrow path until it merges with another path on the riverside; go through a wooden kissing gate and bear right as the paths fork, across the riverside meadows to a gate which leads into 'Woodland Walk'. The route through this reclaimed old industrial area meanders pleasantly on a wooded path via some walkboards to reach the gate where you turn right and emerge by some restored stone buildings. Almost immediately, bear left on the Goyt Way to emerge on a road by some small warehouses beneath New Mills railway station.

The Goyt Way now drops down to the right towards the Millennium Walkway alongside the river. It's easy to see why this impressive structure won an award. Clinging to the wall of one of the country's most vertiginous railway embankments, this is the last important link in the chain of green spaces and walkways along the two rivers that converge underneath New Mills, earning them the title of 'The Park Under The Town'.

New Mills is a fascinating mill town and a visit to the Heritage Centre is recommended – follow the signs to the town centre and the Heritage

Centre is up the steps at the end of the walkway. Don't miss the viewpoint over Torr Mill at the top, by the entrance. Real ale-wise the town is disappointing. It's best to have some non-alcoholic refreshments in the Heritage Centre before pushing on to the delights to come! If you need a beer before leaving town, try the Queens Arms on Church Road, a reliable Robinson's house.

Return to the waterside down the steps and continue left under the viaduct to the confluence with the River Sett – here you can appreciate the geography of the town, sitting on a marked promontory above the two rivers. The ruins here are those of a once significant mill. Follow the River Goyt by taking the path bearing gently to the right over the bridge; the route almost immediately regains its rural feel. The Goyt Way bears 90 degrees right at a farm to join and cross the river by the Goytside Meadows Nature Reserve, then up the path straight ahead to rejoin the canal. Now bear left and follow the towpath for a fair way on past the Furness Vale Marina and a swing bridge until you reach a metal footbridge advertising your next pub, the Dog & Partridge.

Cross the canal here and walk up to emerge on the busy A6 just before roundabout. Cross with great care as visibility is not good, and in the lane opposite and to your left lies the **Dog & Partridge** 3. On a quiet backwater since the A6 was rerouted, the pub offers five beers on handpump including Coach House Gunpowder Mild and Caledonian Deuchars IPA. It's an Enterprise Inns house, offering food lunchtimes and evenings, and welcoming both children and dogs. It also hosts an annual beer festival in August.

Return to the canal the same way and carry

Crossing the Goyt near Strines

on along the canal spur for a very pleasant half-mile stretch up to the Bugsworth Basin (signed). Just beyond lies the **Navigation Inn** , which modestly describes itself as 'probably the best pub in the world'. You can be the true judge of that but the atmospheric interior with its numerous nooks and crannies and a diverse collection of

The interesting Navigation Inn, Buxworth

memorabilia certainly makes for a pleasant experience. Another dog- and child-friendly pub; and food from an extensive menu is available at most times. As for the beers, there's a wide choice, with Taylor Landlord, Theakston Bitter and Marston's Pedigree the fixtures, with rotating guest. Check the web site for more details. The outside areas of this former canalside pub are pleasant but the setting has been compromised by noise from the new road passing close by. Nonetheless it is a rewarding pub that is likely to make a good impression.

To reach Whaley Bridge you could simply return to the canal junction and turn left but I recommend taking the narrow lane from the pub to the left over the main road and forking right at the junction, whereupon it becomes narrower still and quieter, leading you uphill and soon affording fine views over the town. Walk along the road ignoring the footpath signs to your right (unless you're a good map reader) and when the road drops to a junction you'll spot your next pub just down to your right, the **Shepherd's Arms Inn** 5. If you like old-fashioned pubs this is undoubtedly one of the highlights of the area in a real gem of a building: an old-fashioned layout with a proper public bar adorned with venerable old benches and a stone floor. There's a small drinking entrance lobby where locals congregate – it was almost certainly once the off-sales area and now has the nickname of the 'lift shaft'! The lounge to the left is carpeted and retains a period ambience complete with piano. Four handpumps dispense beers from the Marston's and Jennings range. You may well be happy to spend the rest of the day in the Shepherd's, venturing out only to one of the town's numerous oriental eateries (for the Shepherd's only offers lunchtime food) but if you want to move on try the **Navigation** 6 (no relation) in Johnson Street close to the canal basin which is to open all day from noon. Expect Black Sheep Bitter and a guest beer, often Caledonian Deuchars IPA, in a handsome building with a carefully modernised interior, not to mention a rather fancy website.

There are good public transport services back to Stockport and Manchester but if you want to return to Marple after 6.30pm, your best bet might be a taxi to New Mills station where there is an hourly train service.

PUB INFORMATION

1 The Sportsman
105 Strines Road, Strines, Stockport
Cheshire SK6 3AE 0161 427 2888
www.the-sportsman-pub.co.uk
Hours: 12-3, 5-11; Sat 12-11; Sun
12-10.30.
Food: 12-2; 6-9 (Sun 12-8).

2 Fox Inn
Brookbottom, Marple
Cheshire SK22 3AY
Hours: closed Mon; Tue-Thu 12-3;
7-11. Fri-Sun 12-11
Food: lunchtimes until 2 (6 weekends)

3 Dog & Partridge
Bridgemont, Whaley Bridge
Derbyshire SK23 7PB 01663 732284
Hours: Mon-Thu 11-3; 5-11; Fri, Sat
11-11; Sun 12-10.30
Food: Mon-Fri 11.30-2.30; 5-9.45;
Sat 11.30-9.45; Sun 12-9.30

4 Navigation Inn
Brookside, Buxworth, Whaley Bridge
Derbyshire SK23 7NE 01663 732072
www.navigationinn.co.uk

Hours: Mon-Sat 11-Midnight;
Sun 12-11
Food: lunchtime and evenings, all
day in summer.

5 Shepherd's Arms Inn
7 Old Road, Whaley Bridge, Derbyshire SK23 7HR 01663 732384
Hours: Mon 2-12; Tue-Fri 1-12;
Sat & Sun: 12-12.
Food: Mon-Fri 1-2.30; Sat 12-2.30
CAMRA Regional Inventory

6 Navigation
Johnson St, Whaley Bridge
Derbyshire SK23 7LU
01663 719184
www.thenavigation.net
Hours: noon-11 daily

Local attractions: New Mills Heritage
Centre, www.newmillsheritage.com;
Lyme Park, Disley (see www.national-
trust.org.uk); Bugsworth Canal Basin;
Sett Valley Trail (traffic free walking
and cycle route) to Hayfield from New
Mills; Buxton Spa, 8 miles.

macclesfield group

walk 19: Gritstone Trail North via Kerridge and Tegg's Nose

walk 20: Gritstone Trail South via Wincle Minn and Wincle Village

above: **River Dane near Wincle** below: **Sandstone terrace in Wincle**

Gritstone Trail North via Kerridge and Tegg's Nose

WALK INFORMATION

Start/Finish: Spinners Arms, Palmerston Street, Bollington

Access: Bus 392 hourly from Macclesfield (check *Peak District Bus Timetable*). Trains to Macclesfield from all parts

Distance: 6¼ miles (10 km) to the Hanging Gate Inn, 8 miles (13 km) to Langley. OS Map: OL24

The walk: A challenging walk; advisable to make in good weather

The pubs: Hanging Gate Inn, Higher Sutton (963696). Option to visit St Dunstan Inn, Langley

The excellent Gritstone Trail follows the line of the sandstone escarpment guarding the western edge of the Peak and this is one of the best stretches of the route with fine scenery and commanding views in all directions. The walk climbs to over 1,000 feet and much of the route is quite exposed so it's advisable to do the walk in good weather. It also relies on a bus to return to Macclesfield at the end of the walk, so make sure you have your *Peak District Bus Timetable* to hand! Look out for the distinctive Gritstone Trail waymarks with the letter G inside a boot print. This makes navigation on the Gritstone Trail nice and easy, although more care is needed on the last couple of miles of this walk, when off the Trail.

Start at the Spinners Arms (938779) on Palmerston Street, a short distance uphill from one of CAMRA's Regional Inventory pubs, the Holly Bush, and the nearest thing that Bollington has to a High Street. Take the first right beyond the Spinners which ironically is the real High Street, and at the far end by the Red Lion a turn left and continue

View over Bollington, Clarence Mill and beyond from White Nancy

Looking south towards the easily recognised 286-ft high transmitter tower on Croker Hill

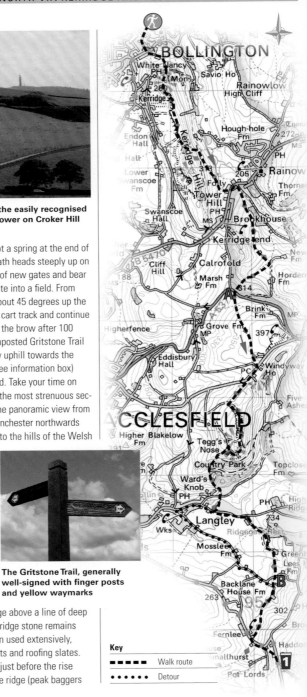

for 100 yards until you spot a spring at the end of the terrace where a footpath heads steeply up on setts. Leave this by a pair of new gates and bear left through the second gate into a field. From here it's best to head at about 45 degrees up the steep slope to join a wide cart track and continue uphill on this to the top of the brow after 100 yards or so where the signposted Gritstone Trail (GT) continues relentlessly uphill towards the obelisk of White Nancy (see information box) which is now visible ahead. Take your time on this stretch for it is by far the most strenuous section of the whole walk! The panoramic view from the top is superb from Manchester northwards across the Cheshire Plain to the hills of the Welsh borderlands and south to the huge and distinctive radio tower on Croker Hill. Close at hand to the east are the moors rising to Shining Tor just left of Rainow, the village down below you.

When you've had a chance to draw your breath continue

The Gritstone Trail, generally well-signed with finger posts and yellow waymarks

southwards along the ridge above a line of deep quarries to your right. Kerridge stone remains highly prized and has been used extensively, particularly for paving setts and roofing slates. Within about half a mile, just before the rise to the highest point on the ridge (peak baggers

Key

- - - - Walk route

• • • • • • Detour

are expected to race to the top and back), the Gritstone Trail leaves the ridge to the left beyond a gate – it's difficult to make it out for the first few yards so follow the wall downhill – and joins up to a decent track revealing excellent scenery as it meanders through trees, dropping steeply towards the village of Rainow below and past the newly excavated ruins of Cow Lane Mill. Like Macclesfield, Rainow's speciality was silk and at one time the village had numerous mills. Today Rainow is probably more renowned for its annual scarecrow festival in July, when you'll be accompanied through the village by all sorts of lifelike mannequins.

Emerging onto the busy road (B5470) turn left and walk past some houses for a couple of minutes. Turn right at the sharp bend and you'll spot a lane opposite climbing the hill (wooden post sign). Take this and in a few yards turn right again on the Gritstone Trail (GT) to climb on to a good track with views back to Kerridge opening up. Keep towards the left hand wall to avoid missing a stile but simply follow the waymarks, ignoring other paths that branch off, until eventually, still climbing, you reach a metal gate stile. Note the Gritstone Trail turns 90 degrees right at this point over another wooden stile. The gradient levels off

Path off Kerridge Ridge towards the small village of Rainow, nestling deep in the folds of the Pennine hills

here and you can enjoy the very fine vista to your right as you walk along this path, still looking out for the GT signs. After a steep drop and climb, you'll emerge at the junction between the busy A537 road and a minor lane (A, ⊛ 947743). Take

The delightful view south to the Langley reservoirs from Tegg's Nose

The distinctive spine of Kerridge Ridge, made of carboniferous sandstone

great care crossing here. You should see the path continuing slightly to the left on a well-defined uphill track. Of interest here is the view ahead to Shutlingsloe, sometimes rather flatteringly called the 'Cheshire Matterhorn', nonetheless it does have a shapely summit which looks rather higher than its 1,640 feet.

Reach the Buxton Old Road by Windway House, and turn right here down towards the Tegg's Nose Visitor centre, keeping an eye out for traffic (although you're soon off the road again and onto a track). There are toilets and a small exhibition centre here, for what was once simply a large quarry is now a Country Park. The

WHITE NANCY

Looking like it was made out of icing or snow, White Nancy was built as a summer house by the Gaskell family of nearby Ingersley Hall, around 1815. It was probably a commemoration of the victory at the battle of Waterloo (1815) and was originally open with an internal chamber and table. However, it was later blocked up due to vandalism.

White Nancy hasn't always been as white as she is now. For much of her existence, her stonework was neither rendered nor painted, and in a poem eulogising Nancy after the Great War, J S Chatterton, a local character, lamented the monument's dilapidated condition:

'...for the signs of decay are upon her
And she's going the way of us all
But I'm sorry she's so much neglected
While standing up here in the cold
I think she deserves better treatment
If only because she is old'

The monument was gifted to the people and nearby village of Bollington as recently as 1999, at which point it was repaired, replastered and repainted. It is certainly a very conspicuous sight, standing as it does at 920 ft above sea level.

White Nancy dominates the skyline around Bollington

Terrace of cottages seen from across Bottoms Reservoir, Langley

Gritstone Trail continues over the highest point of Tegg's Nose – follow the yellow brick road (and the GT signs) from the visitor centre. Just before the highest point you'll see an impressive exposure of the gritstone bands of rock. Numerous information boards emphasise the value of the stone, and there's also a display of cutting and winching gear alongside the path just before you reach a seat and viewpoint. It's easy to see the attraction here as the valley stretches below scattered with farms and looking the very picture of rural life, while away to the south a series of reservoirs adds interest to a gently undulating landscape dotted with trees. Time has healed most of the scars of the quarries. As you walk around the southern end of Tegg's Nose don't miss the GT sign directing you left downhill from the main path. It drops down through a welcome stretch of woodland to the dam of the higher (Tegg's Nose) reservoir and then immediately across the spillway of the lower (Bottoms) reservoir. These reservoirs were built to supply water to the silk mills of Macclesfield. If you're lucky with

the weather, the photogenic terrace of the old cottages will be reflected in the water (it's only close-up that you notice the plastic windows).

The village of Langley with its pub (*St Dunstan Inn*, see below) and bus stop is close by and down the lane to the right if you've run out of time or energy, but the route continues along the lane to

View of Shutlingsloe, known locally as the Matterhorn of Cheshire

the left skirting the Bottoms Reservoir and bearing right on a well-made track just beyond the end of it. A little care is required to follow the trail correctly as it winds up and around a couple of isolated little cottages to emerge on a sunken lane just beyond (B, 953706). Similarly, take care again when following the path beyond the lane as it climbs steadily towards Higher Sutton to emerge on Meg Lane just above the hamlet. Bear left here on Meg Lane for a short distance taking the second

The impressively located 17th-century Hanging Gate Inn

of two footpaths on the right (not the wide lane by the steel gate) which brings you straight out by the **Hanging Gate Inn** 🚩, which if you've judged correctly will be open to welcome you.

The site of this venerable early 17th-century building is almost guaranteed to impress. It stands at 1,089 ft above sea level with massive views westwards. If you arrive, as I have before, with a storm sweeping in over the exposed ridge, you'll be doubly grateful for the sanctuary of the delightful little public bar with its welcoming open fire. Beyond are two other rooms, the further known as the Blue Room – legend has it that the original landlord of the pub used it to spy on lovers. The room has retained its blue

colour and painted eye on the ceiling. The View Room at the far end is used for dining (children are allowed in here). The pub was kept by a one-armed namesake of mine about a century ago and simply known as Tom Steel's and, of course, the establishment has its very own ghost. So, despite much modernisation the thickly walled pub still retains plenty of character and the food comes recommended. Beers are from Hyde's with up to two seasonal guests. The pub sign is most unusual, and has a mysterious little verse…

Allow about 45 minutes to walk back down to Langley for your bus – either retrace your route to the sunken lane and instead of heading to the pub, follow the lane down bearing right at junctions, or walk back down through Higher Sutton on Meg Lane taking the first right fork, then left, then right. If you've time whilst waiting for your bus (and there are plenty of good ale options back in Macclesfield, see your *Good Beer Guide*) the *St Dunstan Inn* in Langley opens at 5pm weekdays (all day weekends) and offers Banks's beer and a guest ale. Bus Service 14 runs hourly except Sundays and bank holidays.

PUB INFORMATION

🚩 **Hanging Gate Inn**
Meg Lane, Higher Sutton
Macclesfield, Cheshire SK11 0NG
01260 252238
Hours: 12-3, 5-11; 12-11 Sat;
12-10.30 Sun
Food: lunchtimes and evenings

Offering a warm welcome to visitors, despite the curt sign, the Hanging Gate Inn

TRY ALSO:

St Dunstan Inn
Main Road, Langley
Macclesfield, Cheshire SK11 0BU
01260 252615
Hours: 5-midnight; noon-midnight
Sat & Sun
Food: has menus for local takeaways

Local attractions: Tegg's Nose Country Park; Adlington Hall (www.adlingtonhall.com), 6 miles; Macclesfield Silk Museums; Jodrell Bank Observatory Visitor Centre, 10 miles.

Gritstone Trail South via Wincle Minn and Wincle Village

WALK INFORMATION

Start/Finish: Rushton Spencer (⊙ 937626)

Access: 108 bus service from Ashbourne, Derby and Macclesfield

Distance: 8½ miles (13.5 km). 5½ miles (9 km) to the Ship. OS Map: Explorer OL24

The walk: An undulating walk at the westernmost edge of the Peak Park, which requires navigational care at times. It can easily be shortened a little if required

The pub: Ship Inn, Wincle

A thoroughly enjoyable circuit at the westernmost edge of the Peak District National Park taking in both a rewarding stretch of the delightful River Dane and a decent climb up onto Wincle Minn affording very fine views all around. With care the navigation should present few problems; quite a long pull up onto the Minn, which is fairly exposed in poor weather. The appealing Ship Inn at Wincle has been sensitively extended of late and now offers a more ambitious range of cask ales, so it's definitely worth getting out of bed for this circuit!

Start at Ruston Spencer on the limited but useful 108 bus service from Ashbourne, Derby and Macclesfield, alighting at the junction of the A523 with Station Lane (⊙ 937626). Walk down the lane until just by the Knot Inn you'll see the old station house. At this point pick up the Staffordshire Way, which follows the old railway track, and head north for about half a mile (the stony surface is hard on the feet). There are good

View of the rolling hills and gorgeous countryside around Wincle

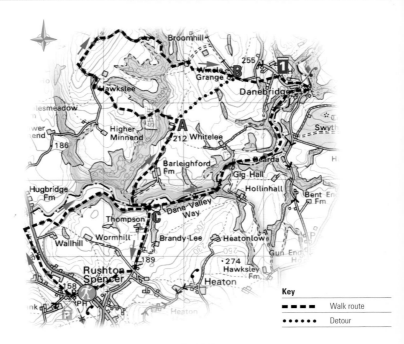

Key

▬ ▬ ▬ Walk route

• • • • • • Detour

views off to the left of the Cloud (1,125 ft), the prominent hill with the pronounced nose, which you'll see for quite a bit of this walk. Where the track ends the path slopes steeply left down to a lane and joins the Gritstone Trail (GT) leading under the bridge and up to the main road (A523). Cross into the meadows following an old river terrace to a stile and then swinging uphill to a bridge over an old conduit. This in fact was a feeder designed to

Selection of handpumps at the Ship Inn

take water from the River Dane to Rudyard Lake, which in turn supplies the Caldon Canal at Leek. Follow the now overgrown conduit to the left (FP sign) and soon the intrusive noise of the busy A523 road recedes and you're in thickly wooded and rolling countryside. After about a mile you reach a kissing gate by a bridge. Here, follow

the GT as it doubles back downhill on a tarred lane to Barleigh Ford Bridge. There's a short steep hill climb beyond, leaving the farm lane almost immediately on a sharp bend following the well-signed GT over a stile and up into glorious countryside to Dumkins (A, ◉ 949648).

If you're pushed for time here, where our route turns 90 degrees left from the tree-canopied path, you could simply go through the stile ahead and follow a good track up through the trees, which undulates in a pretty straight course to rejoin the main route in just over half a mile at Wincle Grange (B, ◉ 955654). Otherwise follow the GT sign left steeply down to Shell Brook and up the far side of the valley, the gradient remaining quite steep for a few hundred yards over a stile keeping to

The Ship Inn, a village pub providing a welcome to walkers and locals alike

the fence on your left. The path becomes well waymarked up to Hawkslee ahead and above. The farm was once worked by the monks from Wincle Grange, which you'll pass later on.

Follow the lane that runs up from the farm (with good views right to Shutlingsloe, the so-called Cheshire Matterhorn – see Walk 19) and in a short distance you reach the southern end of the ridge of Wincle Minn. All of a sudden a tremendous extensive view opens out ahead of you to the west which makes the effort of climbing the hill worthwhile. Across the expanse of the Cheshire Plain you should be able to identify the enormous bowl of the Jodrell Bank Observatory, the crag at Beeston Castle in Tarporley, with even the Clwyd Hills beyond visible on a clear day. Walk along the ridge for a short distance on the very quiet gated road with Croker Hill and its sizeable mast dominating the view left. Just beyond the first gate, turn off to the right (signed), although you could detour 500

yards to the summit and back if you wish. Head down a surprisingly good track to the ruins at Mareknowles where the right of way goes left of the boundary fence and down the hill offering stunning views up the secluded valley of Greaseley Hollow. This heavily wooded valley filled with oak, beech, alder and hazel was once part of the royal hunting forest of Macclesfield, set aside for the recreational pleasure of the Norman kings and barons. Very little of it now remains uncleared.

When you reach the foot of the slope just before the steep drop down to the river, paths lead left and right. Turn right here and follow a very good path leading into what feels like a lost valley and on to a footbridge before climbing directly uphill towards the farm above you. With the house a few yards to your left by another T-junction of paths, turn right and then left, after 50 yards, on a waymarked path making your way uphill, slightly away from the fence. You'll see a stile by a gate – follow the clear track beyond to

Wincle Grange ahead (B,  955654). This historic building, now a farmhouse, was originally constructed by the Monks of Combermere Abbey, near Nantwich, sometime around the year 1500 and was used as a Cistercian priory. Reaching the quiet road here walk along for a couple of minutes in the same direction and, some 100 yards further on, take the footpath that heads to the right at about 45 degrees away from the road straight down into a wonderful beech hanger (a wood clinging to a slope). The footpath, crossing one track, carries on directly down to a road just 50 yards above **The Ship Inn** 🔢.

The Ship is a fine example of the local vernacular style, probably late 16th-century, and its public area has recently been sensitively extended. The wooden-floored public bar with carpeted dining room beyond has been augmented by a tasteful children's room with another dining area beyond that all without compromising the considerable character of the building. Regular beers are Moorhouse's Premier and (unusually for this region) Fuller's London Pride, with two guest ales, usually from the wide range of local microbreweries. Traditional cider is also available.

So, how did a pub so far from the sea come to have the name it does? Sir Philip Brocklehurst, a relative of Sir John of nearby Swythamley Hall, sailed with the explorer Shackleton on one of his many expeditions to the Antarctic, as Assistant Geologist. The pub was renamed in honour of this important local connection, and the sign on one side depicts the Nimrod in Antarctic ice. The other side carries the Brocklehurst coat of arms.

From the Ship it's a simple walk back down

The Ship Inn sign featuring the Nimrod, used in Shackleton's 1908 Antarctic expedition

the delightful Dane Valley. Walk down to the foot of the hill by the bridge and turn right on the wide track by the phone box past Tolls Farm and the fish farm into a well-wooded meadow and simply follow this down until you reach a footbridge. After about 15 minutes this will take you over the river by some weirs. This was the point at which water was drawn off the Dane into the conduit we followed earlier. The path continues (signed to Barleigh Ford Bridge). Between the river and the dry conduit channel you walk past a couple of delightfully sited cottages until you reach the bridge by the kissing gate from which we emerged earlier (C,  945637).

For an alternative route back to Rushton Spencer, head uphill left over the bridge to a hamlet in about seven or eight minutes. Here at the junction of small lanes, with a sign to Wormhill Farm on the right, look for a footpath sign heading off just a few yards on the right which leads you between a hedge and a fence, keeping right of the oak trees. Follow this to the first of several well-built stiles taking the path straight down (ignoring cross paths and tracks) to a large sandstone house. Walk through the yard of the house and along the driveway to the junction where the A523 road is only 50 yards to your left and Station Lane is straight ahead of you.

PUB INFORMATION

🔢 **The Ship Inn**
Wincle, Macclesfield
Cheshire SK11 0QE
01260 227217
Hours: closed Mon (except Bank Hols); 12-3, 6.30 (5.30 Fri)-11; 12-11 Sat; 12-10.30 Sun
Food: lunchtimes and evenings (not Sun evening)

Local attractions: The Roaches (sandstone rock outcrop) and Lud's Church (natural chasm), 4 miles; Tittesworth Reservoir and Visitor Centre, 4 miles; Gawsworth Hall (www.gawsworthhall.com), 5 miles.

hartington group

above: **Hartington** below: **The delights of Dovedale**

Longnor and Earl Sterndale
– the Upper Dove Valley

WALK INFORMATION

Start/Finish: Longnor Market Place

Access: Bus 442 runs from Ashbourne to Buxton via Longnor. OS Map: Explorer OL24

Distance: 4¾ miles (7.5 km)

The walk: A moderately easy circular walk with a couple of steep climbs – may be muddy underfoot in places

The pubs: Quiet Woman Inn, Earl Sterndale; Grapes Hotel, Longnor. Option to visit Horseshoe Inn, Crewe & Harpur Arms, both Longnor

A short circular walk astride the geological divide between the gritstone and limestone country of the Upper Dove Valley. There are a couple of steep hills but overall it's a moderate walk with good views of the sharp limestone peaks of Chrome and Parkhouse Hills. Depending on the weather, some sections may be muddy. When it comes to refreshments, bear in mind that the Quiet Woman doesn't open until noon and there's a chippy in Longnor; check times before setting out!

Start the walk by heading for the church from the Market Place (the little cobbled alleyway past the Red Bull Gallery, formerly a pub, is the obvious route) and once at the church take the footpath (signed) along the right-hand edge of the churchyard and over a stile on the wall. This path takes you down a short steep hill and in no time the village has disappeared, and you are in splendid countryside – the valley in front of you is the Dove, whose more southerly reaches are much better known, when the valley becomes narrower and is known as Dovedale. Here, a curiosity is that on the western side of the valley the geology is gritstone (hence the dark brooding character of the buildings in Longnor) but to the east, it's

Dramatic landscape near Longnor

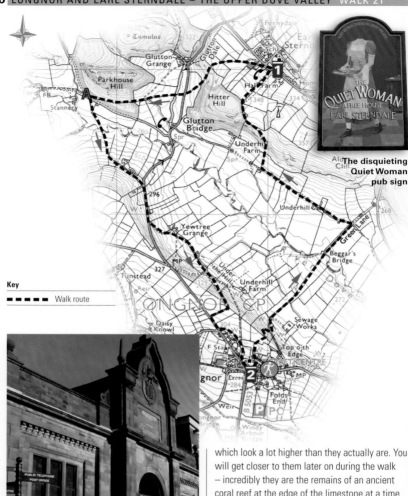

The disquieting
Quiet Woman
pub sign

Key

■ ■ ■ ■ ■ Walk route

The Market Hall, Longnor

light grey limestone. The river marks a boundary, and you should notice the change in the colour of the walls. As you drop down towards the river, a great view opens up to your left of Parkhouse Hill and Chrome Hill, two sharp limestone peaks

which look a lot higher than they actually are. You will get closer to them later on during the walk – incredibly they are the remains of an ancient coral reef at the edge of the limestone at a time when the area was under water.

Cross the river at Beggar's Bridge and walk along the track for a further 300 yards before turning left onto another good track, parallel to the river. On your right the ramparts of the limestone hills rise steeply and, before you reach the appropriately named Underhill Farm in about 10 minutes, a footpath leaves to the right and climbs steeply up the slope, leading with fine views into the village of Earl Sterndale; the path exits right opposite the village green and adjacent to the **Quiet Woman Inn** **1**.

Earl Sterndale is not a pretty village, and has few if any buildings of note, aside from the pub and the church, which has the unfortunate distinction of having been bombed, probably in error, during World War II. It would have been hard to make a living here, high up on the exposed moor, but the farmsteads called 'granges' located hereabouts date back to the time when much of this land was owned by Basingwerk Abbey (a Welsh Abbey near Holywell) and monks inhabited these buildings, working the poor soil.

The inn, the Quiet Woman, is another matter however and remains one of the author's favourites, by virtue of its homely simplicity. The very noteworthy pub sign has the words 'Soft words turneth away wrath' below which is the picture of a decapitated woman! Legend tells us she was Chattering Chatteris, a former publican's wife, who made his life a misery by continual nagging even in her sleep. Eventually the distraught man lopped off her head, with the apparent approval of the erstwhile regulars! A somewhat warmer welcome is assured today, and the interior is pleasantly unspoiled. The main room is unpretentiously furnished, and there's a separate children's room with pool table. Beers are from the Marston's stable and include a mild (Mansfield) with an increasingly ambitious guest beer range. Simple snacks are available at lunchtimes – don't expect a gourmet experience.

Leaving the pub, make as if to return the same way and immediately on scaling the stile pick up another path leading off to the right of the arrival path. This leads you through pastures with walls and stiles back to the edge of the escarpment, with renewed views across to Chrome and Parkhouse Hills. Be warned

Limestone peaks on the way to the village of Earl Sterndale

LONGNOR

Longnor, the starting point of the walk, repays closer inspection. Its centre has an urban feel that belies the actual size of the village – a spacious cobbled market square surrounded by some handsome buildings, for example the red brick Crewe & Harpur Arms, named after the Harpur Crewe family, important local landowners. The truth is that at one time it was a significant settlement with ambition to be a thriving market town, but it was bypassed by the modern rail and road system and today is something of a backwater.

Despite this, it is a vibrant community with a strong identity and a small industrial estate. The interesting market hall, now a craft centre and coffee shop on the square, is a reminder of its former pretensions. Look at the inscription above the entrance, giving the tariffs of long forgotten market tolls. The austere church of St Bartholomew was rebuilt in the 18th century and stands on foundations at least 800 years old. But architecturally Longnor is a place where the whole is greater than the sum of the parts, and it makes a satisfying short stroll to walk around the solid and attractive sandstone buildings arranged compactly around the market square.

that the path drops very steeply down to the dale below, to cross the road close to the curiously named Glutton Bridge. Pick up the path ahead, crossing a small stream and skirting the foot of

The bar at the Quiet Woman Inn with an historic collection of *Good Beer Guide* stickers (right)

the spiky Parkhouse Hill (it's now access land, although if you have spent any time in the Quiet Woman Inn the thought of venturing up might be some way from your mind). Join the small gated road where there's a path cutting back sharply left (A, 078668). If you want to extend your walk, and have a map, the little hamlet of Hollinsclough, a mile further on along the path continuing straight ahead at this point, makes a pleasant walk and destination.

The path recrosses the infant River Dove and ascends back onto the gritstone side of the valley to join the Buxton Road. Turn right and walk carefully along the lane (remember the rule is to walk in single file facing the traffic) for about 250 yards to pick up a path dropping downhill left. This right of way then follows a route parallel to the road, past a couple of farmsteads, to

emerge, about two-thirds of a mile later, back in Longnor village. Consult the map and don't worry if you appear to lose the route – you can't come to too much harm! Alternatively, if it's a little muddy, you might prefer to stick to the road which generally isn't too busy.

In Longnor the **Grapes Hotel** 2, after a period of closure, has re-opened as a real ale free house with Marston's Bitter, Grays Mild and maybe a guest ale or two – so this might be your best bet in the village, although the others are not exactly far away! The *Horseshoe Inn* usually has Marston's beers on tap, and food. The Grapes itself offers bar snacks, but if you need something more substantial try the *Crewe & Harpur Arms* across the square or even the Cheshire Cheese down the street – these days it is more of a food place than a pub.

PUB INFORMATION

1 Quiet Woman Inn
Earl Sterndale, Buxton
Derbyshire SK17 0BU
01298 83211
Hours: 12-3 (4 Sat), 7-11; 12-5, 7-10.30 Sun
Food: lunchtime snacks only
CAMRA Regional Inventory

2 Grapes Hotel
Market Place, Longnor
Buxton, Derbyshire SK17 0NT
01298 83802
Hours: 5 (2 Sat & Sun)-late
(hours may vary: phone ahead)
Food: bar snacks only

TRY ALSO:

Horseshoe Inn
Market Place, Longnor
Buxton, Derbyshire
SK17 0NT
01298 83262

Crewe & Harpur Arms
Market Square, Longnor
Buxton, Derbyshire
SK17 0NS
01298 83205

Local attractions: Longnor Craft Centre (01298 83587); Upper Dove Valley walks.

An 18-century inn, the Crewe & Harpur Arms, Longnor

Hartington's Limestone Dales

WALK INFORMATION

Start/Finish: Hartington village green (128604)

Access: Bus service 442 Buxton to Ashbourne via Hartington (daily). Other less frequent services, see *Peak District Bus Timetable*

Distance: 6½ miles (10.5 km). OS Map: Explorer OL24

The walk: A pretty straight-forward walk – well-signed and generally good under foot, so make the most of the refreshment opportunities

The pubs: Waterloo Inn, Biggin; Hartington Hall Youth Hostel, Charles Cotton Hotel, both Hartington

Probably one of the easiest routes in this book, where the scenery and, indeed, the ales more than repay the effort expended. This less busy section of the Dove is charming in almost all weathers, and you'll have done most of the route by the time you reach the first stop. Hartington also makes an excellent base to try several of the walks in this part of the park.

Start from Hartington village green and head past the market place and down Mill Lane towards Warslow but only for about 125 yards as just between the pottery and the public toilets you'll see a footpath sign leading towards Beresford Dale. Taking this quickly leaves the village behind and soon you're heading through meadows towards the point where the meandering River Dove ahead leaves its wide flood plain and enters a narrow gorge. Charles Cotton, whose name is commemorated in the hotel you've just passed in the village, was a fishing companion of Isaac Walton (author of *The Compleat Angler*, first published 1653). You can see his little fishing lodge across to the right just before you enter the trees, sadly looking rather neglected.

The 17th-century Hartington Hall, now a Youth Hostel

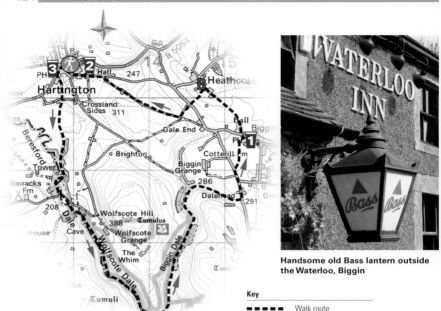

Handsome old Bass lantern outside the Waterloo, Biggin

Key
■ ■ ■ ■ ■ Walk route

Beresford Dale footbridge near Pike Pool

Suddenly you're in the confines of Beresford Dale, with an imposing cliff topped with a tower rising above you across the river. Just beyond by the footbridge is the Pike Pool – referring not to the fish but the striking spike (or pike) of limestone – being the first of many noteworthy features in Dovedale. It's about a further hour's pleasant stroll down the river until you reach a junction where Biggin Dale joins the valley from the left (A, ◉, 142570). When you reach a fork in the path turn up here into another deep and confined valley, this one usually without a stream (see information box), featuring a mixture of hawthorn scrub and open slopes. Carry along the valley and, disregarding the attractive path leading back to Hartington on your left, bear right by the sign to Dale Head in a curving valley which brings you up to a minor public road. Turn left here and, ignoring the sign to Biggin at the junction, carry straight on for another 200 yards to where a sign on the right indicates a footpath across fields to the **Waterloo Inn** **1**.

This is a pleasantly unpretentious local, which would look better without the rather dull rendering. You have a choice of four real ales with a couple from Black Sheep, M&B Mild and a changing guest beer. Food ranges from sandwiches to main meals including Sunday roast. Any children you've brought along can amuse themselves on the pool table, and dogs are welcome too. With two-thirds of the walk completed it's an easy saunter back to Hartington: from the pub a path

Charles Cotton Hotel, Hartington – originally a 17th-century coaching inn

THE DRY VALLEYS OF THE WHITE PEAK

Biggin Dale is a dry valley except during prolonged wet periods when the water table (the upper level of saturation in the permeable rock) rises sufficiently for water to flow on the surface from a resurgence (spring) down the lower half of the Dale. There are several theories as to the origin and formation of dry valleys in chalk and limestone, but it's likely here that large rivers in periglacial conditions (when ice sheets were retreating and the cold conditions froze the pores in the rock making water flow on the surface) may have played a part. Also the presence of larger rivers, like the Dove, cutting down to lower levels has probably helped to lower the water table in surrounding tributaries which don't cut as deeply.

Whatever the cause, the valleys offer a sheltered habitat for many plants and animals – and in Biggin Dale, a National Nature Reserve, conservation is a priority. The grassland is managed by stock grazing and selective gorse cutting. There are some areas of semi-natural ash woodlands with an understory (low-level plant growth) including hazel and hawthorn. At ground level you might spot dog's mercury, wood anemone and the broad-leaved helleborine orchid.

almost immediately on the right will take you up the side of the attached caravan site across fields (bear slightly left) to emerge in the hamlet of Heathcote, which has the air of a place where nothing ever happens. Look out for another footpath sign on the left at Chapel Farm immediately beyond the old chapel, (B, 🔍 147602). Go straight through the farmyard bearing slightly right to a gate in the corner by some trees (ignoring another footpath sign leading sharp right), and simply walk downhill to the lane. Almost opposite follow the stony track for a couple of minutes to a good cycle track to Hartington.

Turning right on this track will bring you out in less than a mile right by **Hartington Hall 2**, a very impressive building indeed which has

Limestone cliffs along the river in Wolfscote Dale

Waterloo Inn, Biggin catering for a good mix of locals and visitors to the Peaks

been a youth hostel for most of the last century. If you haven't been in one for some time this is not a youth hostel as you might remember it. Not only does it serve award-winning food but also, believe it or not, fine draft beers sourced from local micro-breweries – a far cry from my first visit back in 70s when I surreptitiously smuggled in a can of something or other (probably Watneys) in the bottom of my rucksack! What's more, the place is open to non-residents, although it's not a bad option for accommodation either.

The village centre is another quarter of a mile down the hill, and whether or not you're staying at the hostel, a visit to the **Charles Cotton Hotel 3** is a must for its excellent selection of up to five locally-sourced ales. The enthusiastic management has put the place very much on the beer map with the local Hartington Bitter and IPA from Whim brewery usually available together with Leatherbritches and maybe Thornbridge beers. It's a welcome new addition to the Peak District's steadily improving real ale scene, and another good accommodation option. If you're using Hartington as a base for other walks there's an easy walk up the Dove valley to Longnor (see Walk 21).

PUB INFORMATION

1 Waterloo Inn
Main Street, Biggin
Buxton, Derbyshire SK17 0DH
01298 84284
Hours: 12-4, 6.30-11;
12-midnight Fri-Sun
Food: 12-2.30; 12-9 Sat & Sun

2 Hartington Hall Youth Hostel
Hall Bank, Hartington
Buxton, Derbyshire SK17 0AT
0870 770 5848

Local attractions: Hartington Hall, good centre for cycle trails (see pp141–5); Buxton Spa, 10 miles.

3 Charles Cotton Hotel
Market Place, Hartington
Buxton, Derbyshire SK17 0AL
01298 84229
Hours: 11-11 daily
Food: all day every day

A fine selection of real ales at the Waterloo Inn, Biggin

The bar at Hartington Hall Youth Hostel

Dovedale and Alstonefield from the Tissington Trail

WALK INFORMATION

Start/Finish: Alsop-en-le-Dale station car park (🔾 156549), or Alstonefield (🔾 130556)

Access: Bus service 442 via Alstonefield; infrequent buses on A515 (check *Peak District Bus Timetable*) and access by cycle from Ashbourne

Distance: About 8 miles (12 km) for full round. Allow 4½ hours including stops. OS Map: Explorer OL24

The walk: A versatile circular walk with more than one starting place. Some steep climbs mean this is not one for the unfit

The pubs: George, Alstonefield. Option to visit Watts Russell Arms, Hopedale

Taking in a cross-section through the popular Dovedale, avoiding the very busy southern end and instead enjoying the side dry valleys, this is limestone country at its best. The route here is described from Alsop on the Tissington Trail and the A515, but an obvious alternative starting point is Alstonefield itself, which also offers accommodation. An early start from here, perhaps with the optional short cut, would see you back in the village in good time for lunch. From Alsop set off by 11am at the latest for a comfortable lunch stop in the George.

From Alsop-en-le-Dale station car park (don't be fooled, the last train ran 40 years ago!) start on the trail and walk northwards keeping an eye out for cyclists on this popular route. Take the second footpath sign on the left after about 15 to 20 minutes walking – it's just before an overbridge in front of you. The waymarked path leads you steeply down into a typical limestone dry valley, which you'll probably have all to yourself. Head left downhill to the foot of the dale where you'll be pleased

View across the popular Dove Valley from Alsop

Well-signed footpath at the bottom of Hall Dale

Stile and path through a typical limestone valley near Alsop

to meet the River Dove at Coldeaton Bridge. A short cut here for the athletic and thirsty is to cross by the footbridge and climb a remorselessly steep bank and at the top follow a track straight into Alstonefield after about a mile… however, under normal circumstances take my advice and

follow the river downstream for about half an hour through very attractive scenery (the latter part on a very quiet lane) as far as the little hamlet of Milldale. This pleasant spot is something of a honeypot for visitors with refreshments (non-alcoholic), toilets and a small National Trust Visitors' Centre. Count yourself lucky if you get here before the daytrippers arrive in force!

Drawing breath leave by the narrow lane past the phone box and postbox up from the confectioners (there's another even steeper path which dives up the bank immediately past the phone box, but you wouldn't thank me for recommending it). Both paths lead into the village of Alstonefield, past St Peter's Parish Church and deposit you squarely on the village green opposite the enviably-sited **George** **1**.

A well-proportioned 16th-century house suggesting former importance, the George looks the part. A corridor leads to a fine bar room on the right, divided into two small areas, the nearer with tiled floor and open fire. Children are welcome here and in the room to the left, which is more given over to eating. There's a wide menu available up to 2.30pm and in the evenings until 9pm. It's a Marston's house so expect the likes of Pedigree and Marston's Bitter with one guest ale (from Black Sheep Brewery on my last visit).

If the ever-popular George is shut or packed beyond tolerance, you could walk down the lane to Hopedale to try the **Watts Russell Arms** . It's getting on for three-quarters of a mile, however, and it's strongly recommend that you phone ahead to ensure that its open. Timothy Taylor Landlord and Black Sheep Bitter are regulars, with the occasional guest beer. (If you do this you can rejoin the route by taking the lane sharp left out the pub towards Milldale and joining the bridleway in a third of a mile just beyond some cottages on the left.)

From the door of the George head to your right and, by Brambles Barn across the road from the green, you'll see a footpath sign which leads you through a squeezer stile and into some fields. Cross the fields by gates and stiles and over a step stile into a larger field with a glorious panorama ahead to and beyond the hamlet of Stanshope. Make straight ahead for the single tree, cutting across to join the wall to your right and then follow the walls as they funnel you through a gate and steeply down to the quiet lane in Milldale. Refugees from the Watts Russell

Hall Dale, a beautiful dry valley leading down to the famous Dovedale

The enticing Watts Russell Arms, Hopedale

Arms rejoin here. As walkers well know, what comes down must go up – so take the walled lane almost opposite and up into Stanshope.

At the road junction (A, ⊛ 128542) bear immediately left by the footpath sign onto a track and then in 100 yards right by another sign for 'Dovedale via Hall Dale'. The dale itself is visible ahead and the path is very easy to follow – a long descent through charming scenery until eventually you reach the River Dove once again.

The George, Alstonefield

Limestone crags of Pickering Tor, Dovedale

It's a pleasant 400 yards detour downstream to the footbridge by the striking pinnacle of Ilam Rock on your right and the jagged crags of Pickering Tor across the river – often dotted with climbers. Once over the footbridge retrace your steps upstream and in a few minutes you'll reach the impressive caves at Dove Holes.

When you get just beyond (B, ⊙, 143536), it's decision time: the route back to Alsop goes right here but if you started from Alstonefield you have the shorter and easier option of following the river upstream back to Mill Dale in less than a mile. Heading for Alsop, Nabs Dale, as the side valley is called, is another typical steep-sided dry valley running into the deeply incised Dovedale. You may well feel you deserve a rest on the slopes if you've done the whole circuit, and why not? The scenery is delightful and the air is filled with birdsong. At the top of the dale, bear left for a sign and stile 50 yards above the farm gate and aim for the telegraph pole. Through another stile and you'll see a footpath sign at the top end of the farm track which you should follow towards Alsop-en-le-Dale, uphill to the crest of the rise where you are again rewarded with a wonderful panorama. Look hard left for the pleasant village of Wetton in the distance; Dovedale (or more properly Wolfscote Dale as it is called in this stretch) is below you and the A515 road straight ahead. Carry on down this unfenced farm lane and straight across the field at the bottom of it to emerge right by Alsop station and car park.

PUB INFORMATION

1 George
Alstonefield, Ashbourne
Staffordshire DE6 2FX
01335 310205
www.s229784751.websitehome.
co.uk
Hours: 11-3, 6-11;
11-11 Sat; 12-10.30 Sun
Food: 12–2.30, 7–9
(not Sun eve)

2 Watts Russell Arms
Hopedale, Alstonefield
Ashbourne, Staffordshire
DE6 2GD
01335 310126
www.wattsrussell.co.uk
Hours: please ring for details

The striking sign of the George

leek group

above: **Stone cottage in Ford** below: **Consall Station**

The Churnet Valley Woodlands and Caldon Canal from Froghall

WALK INFORMATION

Start/Finish: Froghall Wharf (⌖ 026477)

Access: Clowes bus services 234/235/236 links Leek and Cheadle via Froghall and Ipstones

Distance: 7 miles (11.2 km). OS Maps: Explorer 259 (small fragment on OL24)

The walk: A good length walk with some steep climbs but nothing too difficult

The pubs: Black Lion, Consall Forge; Marquis of Granby, Ipstones; Fox & Goose, Foxt

A circuit full of variety in the beautiful and well-wooded Staffordshire Moorlands not far from Alton Towers. Paths are mostly in good condition, well-signed and easy to follow. A couple of steep pulls, notably up the Devil's Staircase out of the Churnet Valley, but not a difficult walk. Trains run on the Churnet Valley Railway most weekends and at some other times – a pleasant addition to the walk, or even an alternative to the first section to Consall. See www.churnetvalleyrailway.co.uk.

Start at Froghall Wharf just north of the junction of the A52 and B5053. Pick up the towpath across the road from the café and immediately you're into a pleasant wooded stretch which leads to a short tunnel under the B5053. Cross the road and rejoin the towpath, simply following it for about 2 miles along the deep and well-wooded Churnet Valley (unless you want to do this stretch by train – see introduction). It's an easy

Froghall Wharf on the Caldon Canal

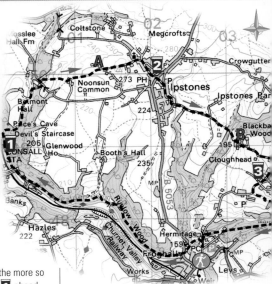

The refurbished interior of the Marquis of Granby

Key

- - - - - Walk route

and pleasant stroll along the canal, the more so since at 11.30am the **Black Lion 1** ahead will be open. It's just beyond Consall station and occupies an enviable location with the river, railway and canal (but no public road) running along the valley outside its front door. The handsome brick building has retained a good deal of character inside; and the garden, which slopes down to the railway, catches the early morning sun. Moorhouse's Blond Witch is a regular beer here, along with Mansfield Cask and occasional guest beers, sometimes from Slaters. If the weather is good, you'll definitely want to linger here and maybe stay for lunch. Be aware that children and dogs are not permitted inside the pub. However, there is a sheltered gazebo outside.

The handsome Marquis of Granby at Ipstones

From the Black Lion climb out of the valley via the very steep and aptly named Devil's Staircase. The well-constructed and signed path leaves at the right hand side of the pub as you emerge, and makes relatively light work of the steep gradient up onto the plateau high above the Churnet with a very steep wooded slope and the sound of running water far below you. The path comes out on the driveway to Belmont Hall; and after about 200 yards downhill leaves this for an attractive trail on your right through woods by a stream emerging by a heavily modernised old chapel on a public lane (Belmont Road). Turn left here and look for a footpath sign on the right after about 150 yards. There is no obvious track across the field here but make for the farm above and 45 degrees to the right of you. Following this line will bring you to the first of a series of waymarked stiles and from here the path is well-signed skirting the farm on the left and continuing beyond with wide views all around. Walk past Oddo Hall (A, ⊚ 014502) and in no time you'll reach St Leonard's parish church sitting at the top end of the village of Ipstones. Turn first right beyond the church and in five minutes you'll arrive in the village centre, where the substantial-looking **Marquis of Granby**  is open all day.

For somebody who frequently moans about insensitive pub refurbishments, I found the Marquis a pleasant surprise. It has just completed a major refit but in a light, modern style throughout resulting in a wooden floor in the bar and quarry tiles in the dining area. The licensee offers beers from her own Belvoir brewery as well as interesting guest ales, so it's a real treat for beer lovers. There's an extensive and wide-ranging menu (available all day from 9am!) if you didn't eat at the Black Lion.

The substantial village of Ipstones still has four pubs but I recommend continuing the walk by heading across the main road into Brookfields Road and following this downhill past the Sea Lion pub (only open evenings at present) and about 200 hundred yards beyond the double dog-leg in the lane (by No. 75) a footpath sign directs you left down to a tarred bridleway, more like a narrow lane. The tarmac gives way to stones and at a cattle grid fork left on a signed narrow wooded path down to a tiny stream. Follow the path up through the woods bearing left when a sign directs you up a walled path (which seems

Consall station, restored to some of its original Victorian charm

CALDON CANAL

The Caldon Canal runs from the basin at Froghall to Etruria near Stoke where it joins the Trent and Mersey Canal. It was opened by the Trent and Mersey Canal Company in 1778 and together with the connecting plateways – a sort of railway where the wide wheels were kept on the flat iron tracks by L-shaped upstands on the running plates – was primarily designed to carry limestone from the productive quarries at Caldon Low a few miles away, to supply water to the Trent and Mersey Canal and to service the small Cheadle coalfield nearby. In the 1920s the major limestone contract was lost and ownership passed to the railways and by the 1950s commercial traffic had largely ceased. Threatened with closure in the 60s it was finally reopened to navigation in 1974. This walk starts by following the canal and ends on the line of the old railway which brought the stone down to the wharf. There's a small information centre which sells refreshments at the wharf open mid-May to early September.

Froghall Wharf, once a hive of industrial activity now a pleasant visitor attraction

The Black Lion pub with enviable views over the canal, river and railway

to double as a tiny stream!) to Shay House at the top (B, ⊚ 032491) where the tarmac takes over again. This track (Shay Lane) leads straight to the rather gaunt looking church at Foxt, where it's a case of turning right and walking downhill to reach the **Fox & Goose** ③. This is a very smart and heavily modernised pub where, although the emphasis is on food, you'll also be able to get a choice of between three and five ales, usually including Greene King Abbot and Bass, with guest beers. It might be worth phoning ahead to double check times.

Continue downhill on the village road for a short distance and at the second bend on a

wooded corner carefully cross and take the good track on the left with a 'Moorlands Walk' way-mark. This path follows the contours above the steep valley below and for the next 10 minutes or so offers the best views on this walk before dropping steeply down over a stile (keep close to the walled boundary). Carry on and over the stream at the bottom before rising through more very appealing woodland and emerging on the track bed of the old inclined plane of the railway, next to a remarkably well-made little pedestrian tunnel. This straight former rail route was in fact the fourth and last attempt to link the three-mile distance between Caldonlow Quarry and Froghall Wharf, and ran from 1847 to about 1920. The Quarries were some 700 ft higher than the wharf, hence the need for steep gradients and inclined planes. It's a walk of just over half a mile down the slope back to the wharf. Note the old wharf cottage and the remains of what was probably the weighing shed almost at the foot of the incline and the massive sandstone blocks, which would have supported the winding gear to haul the wagons up the incline.

Hamps and Manifold – A Circuit from Onecote

WALK INFORMATION

Start/Finish: Onecote village (⊙ 049552)

Access: Very limited public transport – see *Peak District Bus Timetable*

Distance: 9½ miles (15 km), (6½ miles via short cut); OS map: Explorer OL 24

The walk: A circular walk in an open landscape with extensive views. In a quieter corner of the national park, the walk can easily be shortened and the gradients are not too demanding

The pubs: Black Lion Inn, Butterton; Red Lion Inn, Waterfall; Jervis Arms, Onecote

This circular walk is mainly on limestone country, and lies in a less frequented but nonetheless very attractive part of the National Park. Gradients are on the whole gentle and underfoot conditions good. There are some stunning views over the limestone scenery of the Manifold Valley before returning along the upper parts of the river Hamps back to Onecote, where the Jervis Arms is a classic country pub. The walk can easily be shortened if desired. Note the restricted opening hours at the pubs and plan accordingly.

Start in Onecote village – parking is not easy on the main road although there is a minor lane (Douse Lane) joining from the west. Walk northwards along the B5053 for about 400 yards taking the very greatest care since there are no footpaths. Take the metalled lane (Titterton Lane) running off to the right uphill past Home Farm and after a couple of hundred yards carry straight on at the FP sign instead of following the lane to the right. You gain height quickly accompanied by a line of telegraph poles until just beyond a ruin where a path and stiles take you over

Impressive stone house in the pretty hamlet of Ford

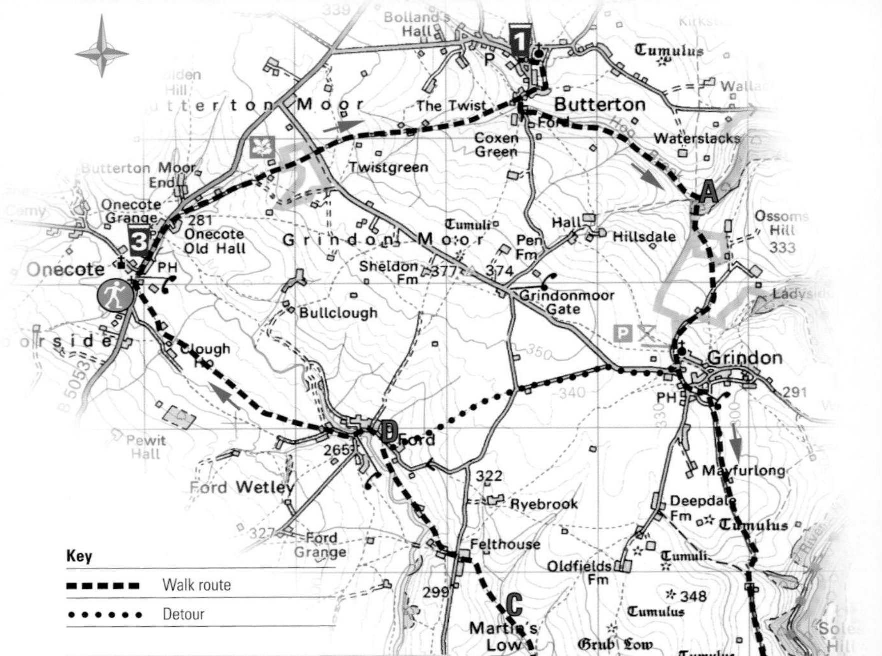

Key

▬ ▬ ▬ ▬ Walk route

• • • • • • Detour

Black Lion Inn, Butterton

a small, unenclosed area of National Trust access land. This is the remains of Grindon Moor, a small area of heather moorland in an area which has been improved over the years for stock rearing. At the summit Parsons Lane is well over 1,000 ft high and you get good views both behind you towards the gritstone areas of Staffordshire and ahead to the Derbyshire limestone, with the spire of Butterton church shortly coming into view.

Go across the lane, through the gate opposite and walk down the stony track to gates by some corrugated iron buildings with yet more great views ahead. Carry on straight down the steep slope keeping close to the tree boundary on your right, past a ruin and below that a house, picking up a grassy track over numerous stiles and gates down into the lower part of Butterton village. With any luck you'll emerge on a tiny lane which doubles as a stream bed in a picturesque setting with a short but very steep climb to your left bringing you up into the village where you'll have no difficulty finding the **Black Lion Inn 1**.

It's an atmospheric free house with a separate dining room (where children can eat with you until 9.30pm) and a good range of four constantly changing real ales. The place also offers accommodation (2 doubles and a family room) which might make an appealing prospect if you're looking for a base for this walk. Ask about the oversized clothes peg sign outside!

Leaving the pub, return to the valley bottom where you want to pick up the path which follows the small Hoo Brook downstream for about three quarters of a mile. The start of the footpath is not clear: the most foolproof way is to climb the lane 300 yards or so uphill and turn left opposite Coxon Green Farm (FP sign) but then double back straight down the field to meet the brook

Idyllic garden at the Jervis Arms, Onecote

where there's a path. It's now plain sailing on a delightful route into a deep limestone valley. It is, however, likely to be muddy in places, as it's also popular with the local cattle. Reach the major junction of footpaths by the footbridge (A, 087555) and take the good bridleway to the right steeply uphill towards Grindon, emerging on a tiny lane with wide views in all directions. A gentle climb to the right is followed by five minutes downhill into Grindon, past the church, which is a little disappointing close-up.

Here, head down to the right beyond the church and then left at the small village green on the lane signed 'Manifold Valley'.

If you want to take a short cut here, consult your map and you'll see a direct route by lane and footpath that will take you westwards to Ford (see below) in little over a mile. Otherwise, a short distance further down the lane on the right hand side, the double fronted detached

The Manifold Valley, home to some impressive karst landscapes

house was until very recently the 'Cavalier', Grindon's pub. It's yet another casualty of the changing social and economic pressures which are forcing pubs out of business in both rural and urban areas.

Another 100 yards or so further on by a bungalow, take a wide stony track (Fleets Lane) heading off to the left. It winds round southwards offering absolutely stunning views across the Manifold Valley, and at the top of the rise ahead equally good prospects to the south. In good weather you'll feel almost as if you're on top of the world here, and chances are you'll have it all to yourself.

Stay on this good path which merges with a bridleway past a farm and onto a tarred lane curving around gently downhill to reach a minor road junction by the stream (B, 083519). Follow the lane to the right (Hays Lane) alongside the stream for a hundred yards or so, taking the signed footpath left over the footbridge and uphill towards the church ahead. The path navigates some nettles before diving through a squeezer stile into the churchyard, at the other end of which you'll see the **Red Lion Inn** **2** 150 yards across an unkempt field to your right. There is actually a right of way directly to the pub through here. The Red Lion offers Bass as a regular, and one or two changing guest beers, sometimes from local micro-breweries. A tempting menu includes locally sourced options. Well-behaved children and dogs are welcome.

The route from here to Ford needs a little more care: leave the pub and walk to your left downhill (Townend Lane and then round to the right on to Hays Lane) to the valley of the little stream you left earlier where a small lane leads off to the left by a house. Follow this quiet little lane as it deteriorates into a track, crosses the now tiny stream just beyond a pond and then through a couple of stiles keeping in the same direction through cow pasture with the river below you on the left. Find a stile and the gate (C,  074527) and afterwards cross the stream on stepping stones to head straight up the spur of high ground ahead of you (don't expect a track!) making for the large red house (Felthouse on the map) which soon appears. Go through the gates to join a minor road. Turn right here and after 50 yards turn left down a concrete farm track between the farm buildings. Just at the end of the buildings where the land falls away steeply in front, and by a FP sign pointing left, turn 90 degrees right on an initially very indistinct line at the back of a ruin (currently under restoration) to pick up a stile through nettles giving great views ahead. This path soon emerges on a 4-WD track taking you down to a small hamlet.

The difficulties almost over, take the path through the first gate and round to the right of some outhouses, beyond which a poor track leads off left of a ruin with the river on your left. Then, keeping the field boundary on your right over the next meadow, re-emerge on the minor lane at

Another one bites the dust: The Cavalier, Grindon, now just another upmarket rural property

Ford by the point where the short cut route (see above) rejoins (D,  067538). (If this sounds a bit tricky, simply keep on the lane at Felthouse and turn left at the T-junction to get to the same point – you won't be bothered with traffic.) Now continue westwards along the lane past some attractive buildings on your right, and after crossing the stream on a bridge turn right at a 'No through road' sign and telephone box. Now it's pretty much a straight route on a tarred lane for the first few hundred yards. Ignore footpath signs right and left and keep ahead as the road becomes a grassy track, uneven and wet in places, to reach the B5053 just south of Onecote. The **Jervis Arms** **3** is about 350 yards on the left, (but again, take care on account of the lack of footways).

A well-run roadside pub with a choice riverside garden, the Jervis is a country pub worth seeking out. The comfortable and characterful interior includes a family room where you can enjoy wide-ranging food and beer menus. The latter includes Titanic Iceberg along with Wadsworth 6X and up to four changing guest beers. Interestingly, you can also try Moravka, an unpasteurised Czech-style pilsner brewed with very few beer miles attached, since it comes not from Prague but from nearby Blackwell Hall in the Peak Park. The quality of the cellarmanship has earned the pub a regular appearance in the *Good Beer Guide*.

PUB INFORMATION

1 Black Lion Inn
Butterton, Leek
Staffordshire ST13 7SP
01538 304232
www.blacklioninn.co.uk
Hours: 12-2 (not Mon), 7-11.30;
12-11 Sun
Food: lunchtimes and evenings
(ring to check times)

2 Red Lion Inn
Waterfall, Waterhouses
Stoke-on-Trent, Staffordshire
ST10 3HZ
01538 308279
www.peaklion.co.uk
Hours: 6.30 (8 Mon)-11; 12-3,
6.30-11 Sat; 12-4, 7-10.30 Sun

Food: no food Mon; 12-2, 6.30-9;
12-3, 7-8.30 Sun evening)

3 Jervis Arms
Onecote, Leek
Staffordshire ST13 7RU
01538 304206
Hours: 12-3, 7 (6 Sat)-midnight;
12-10.30 Sun
Food: 12-2, 7-9.30 daily

Local attractions: Blackbrook
Zoological Park, 2 miles
(www.blackbrookzoo.co.uk); Churnet
Valley Railway (see Walk 24), 6 miles;
Brindley Mill, Leek, 7 miles (www.
brindleymill.net); Cheddleton Flint
Mill, 10 miles.

Enjoying the Tissington Trail

Cycle routes

The Peak District's traffic-free cycle tracks are among the best in the country and as well as offering great family friendly off-road cycle routes they also make good walking options. Here, we recommend some good drinking venues close to the three White Peak trails.

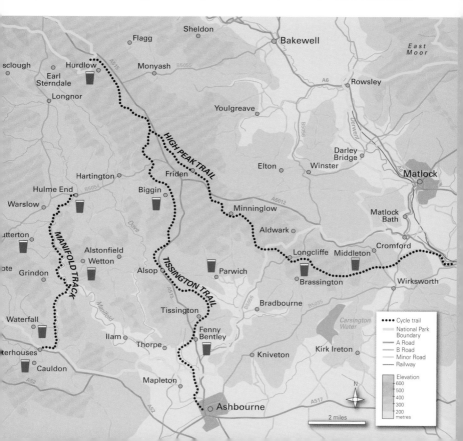

Route 1: **The High Peak Trail**

The 17-mile long High Peak Trail was originally conceived as a canal at the outset of the railway era but built as a railway on canal principles, with contoured sections linked by inclined planes, none steeper than the route starting at High Peak Junction near Cromford up onto the plateau at Middleton Top (also the official start of the new Pennine Bridleway). This also makes a good walk in the reverse direction starting from Middleton Top: you could head north along the canal for a mile from High Peak Junction and sample the pubs in Cromford.

CYCLE INFORMATION

Start: Cromford

Finish: Hurdlow

Cycle hire: at Middleton Top (🔍 275552) and Parsley Hay (🔍 147638)

Access: Trent-Barton Bus R6.1 to the Rising Sun for Middleton Top. There are car parks at Parsley Hay, Minninglow (🔍 194583) and Middleton Top

Connecting walks: 4, 6 & 7

Waterloo Inn, at Biggin

One of the most interesting sections of the Trail is near the scenic Black Rocks, just before Middleton Top, and a walk or bus ride from the Trail into Wirksworth offers several refreshment options.

A stones throw from the Trail to the north, and five minutes down the lane from Middleton Top, is the **Rising Sun Inn**, which welcomes walkers and cyclists, and is open all day from noon. Food is available to wash down the range of ales, usually mainly from national brewers, but beer festivals occur quite regularly where all sorts of interesting local beers surface. There is a garden, and the pub offers accommodation.

Set off westwards from Middleton Top and soon the wonderful countryside of the Peak's limestone plateau opens up just before you pull up the Hopton incline, formerly the country's steepest unaided railway gradient at 1:14. Beyond the rugged outcrops of Harboro' rocks you can leave the Trail at Longcliffe and drop a mile downhill (on a fairly quiet lane but maybe unsuitable for young children) to Brassington, an old lead mining village. Here you'll find the splendidly atmospheric **Olde Gate Inn**, a National Inventory entry with a gleaming old range and wooden tables in the stone-flagged bar. Food is available but children under ten are confined to the beer garden at the rear. Beers are from the Marston's range with a guest. Brassington's other pub, the **Miners Arms**, is worth a visit too.

Return to the Trail and continue west with stunning views southwards. About 12 miles from Middleton you'll reach the junction with the Tissington Trail at Parsley Hay (with a cycle-hire centre and refreshments). Two miles further north and right on the Trail is the **Royal Oak** at Hurdlow. This is the ideal spot if you're out with the family as children are welcome throughout the pub – even on the pool table in the cellar – and catered for on the menu. There are outside lawns with seating if it's warm enough here at a height of over 1,000-ft! Beers are Bass, Marstons and a guest.

PUB INFORMATION

The Rising Sun
26 Rise End, Middleton
Matlock, Derbyshire
DE4 4LS
01629 822420
www.therisingsuninn.biz

Olde Gate Inn
Well Street, Brassington
Derbyshire DE4 4HJ
01629 540448
CAMRA National Inventory

Miners Arms
Miners Hill, Brassington
Derbyshire DE4 4HA
01629 540222

Royal Oak
Hurdlow, Nr Buxton
Derbyshire SK17 9QJ
01298 83288
www.royaloakpub.org
Hours: Tue-Sun noon-11
Food: served noon-9

Route 2: **The Tissington Trail**

The 13-mile route from the junction with the High Peak Trail at Parsley Hay to Ashbourne was originally part of the Buxton to Ashbourne railway, built by the London & North Western Railway (LNWR) and opened in 1899. In its heyday, it carried express trains from Manchester to London and milk from Peak District farms into the capital. Today, the traffic-free leafy trail is perfect for cyclists.

CYCLE INFORMATION

Start: Parsley Hay

Finish: Ashbourne

Cycle hire: at Ashbourne, and at Parsley Hay

Access: buses to Ashbourne from all parts: see *Peak District Bus Timetable*. Irregular services to Parsley Hay listed here also. Car parking at Parsley Hay and in Ashbourne

Connecting walks: 22

Starting from Parsley Hay, head south through the deep cutting and in about 2 miles you'll find the old Hartington signal box. It's worth consulting your map here before heading off the trail either to the **Waterloo Inn** at Biggin, very close to the Trail, or to Hartington beyond. Biggin's unpretentious Waterloo Inn offers four real ales (Black Sheep beers, M&B Mild, and a guest) and food, and welcomes accompanied children (who may enjoy the pool table) until 10pm.

More adventurous riders will enjoy the circular detour on charming quiet lanes to Parwich, a little further south east. This well-heeled village has some fine houses nestling under the limestone plateau, and the **Sycamore Inn**, a pleasantly unspoiled Robinson's two-roomed house. Food is available and children welcome (there's also a playground adjacent).

Find the road out to Alsop-en-le-Dale, another delightful lane although there's a bit of a climb to rejoin the trail just south of the junction with the busy A515 (take care). Ashbourne is still several miles south but on the way there's the quiet estate village of Tissington with its appealing tea rooms, and beyond at Fenny Bentley, (⊙ 177495) off the Trail on the busy A515, is the **Coach and Horses** (Marstons), whilst the nearby **Bentley Brook Inn**, with its extensive garden, is also worth a look.

PUB INFORMATION

Waterloo Inn
Main Street, Biggin
Nr Buxton
Derbyshire SK17 0DQ
01298 84284

Sycamore Inn
Parwich, Ashbourne
Derbyshire DE6 1QL
01335 390212

Coach and Horses
Fenny Bentley, Ashbourne
Derbyshire DE6 1LB
01335 350246

Bentley Brook Inn
Fenny Bentley, Ashbourne
Derbyshire DE6 1LF
01335 350278
www.bentleybrookinn.co.uk

Cyclists enjoying a well-maintained cycle trail

Route 3: **The Manifold Track**

Behind the Crown Inn at Waterhouses (⊙ 085503), the trackbed of the former Manifold Light Railway runs for 9 miles through a deep wooded valley. There are few distant views but the valley scenery is excellent. If you like quirky pubs do not miss the famous old **Yew Tree Inn** at Cauldon, (⊙ 076493) before you set off. It's incongruously sited by the cement factory close to the southern end of the trail but with an amazing interior full of all sorts of knick-knacks. Bass and Burton Bridge beers are the usual fare and there's a family room.

CYCLE INFORMATION

Start: Waterhouses

Finish: Hulme End

Cycle hire: at Waterhouses (on A523) at southern end of track

Access: limited bus services to Waterhouses and Hulme End: see *Peak District Bus Timetable*; car parks at either end of the trail

Connecting walks: 3 & 25

Heading north from Waterhouses you could try an early call at the **Red Lion Inn** at Waterfall, with Bass, M&B Mild and a usually interesting guest ale; see Walk 25 for pub details. Other pub options en route to Hulme End involve quite punishing ascents so either leave your bike in the valley or be prepared for a push! However, neither the traditional **Black Lion** at Butterton nor the **Royal Oak** at Wetton will disappoint – as long as you telephone ahead to ensure they're open!

The section of the route between Wetton Mill and Swainsley, although quiet, is open to vehicles, so you will need to supervise children.

At Hulme End the well-sited **Manifold Hotel** is a few yards from the start of the trail and

Black Lion, Butterton

does offer some interesting ales from local micros, if you're lucky, although it's quite heavily food oriented and seems more interested in drivers than cyclists.

PUB INFORMATION

Yew Tree Inn
Cauldon, Waterhouses
Staffordshire ST10 3EJ
01538 308348

Red Lion Inn
Waterfall, Waterhouses
Staffordshire ST10 3HZ
01538 308 279
Hours; Mon 8-11; Tue-Fri
6.30-11; Sat noon-3, 6.30-11;
Sun noon-4, 7-10.30.
Food: noon-2 (3 Sun),
6.30-9 (7-8.30 Sun).
No food Mondays
www.peaklion.co.uk

Black Lion
Wetton Road, Butterton
Staffordshire
ST13 7SP
01538 304232

Hours: Mon 7-11.30; Tue-Sat
noon-2, 7-11.30; Sun noon-11.
Food: until 1.30 lunchtime,
7-9 evenings
www.blacklioninn.co.uk

Royal Oak
Wetton, Nr Ashbourne
Derbyshire DE6 2AF
01335 310287
Hours: Tues from 8pm
(no food); Weds–Fri
noon–2:30, 7–11;
Sat-Sun noon–3, 7–10:30.
Children in lounge only.

Manifold Hotel
Hulme End
Staffordshire
SK17 0EX
01298 84537
www.themanifoldinn.co.uk

The Manifold Track with Thor's Cave behind

CYCLE HIRE

Ashbourne
Mapleton Lane, Ashbourne
Derbyshire DE6 2AA
01335 343156
email: cyclehire@peakdistrict.gov.uk

Opening hours: 9.30-5.30
(or dusk if earlier)
January: open weekends only
February: open 2-3, 9-24
March-October: open
every day
November: 1-11, 17-18, 24-25
December: closed

Middleton Top
Middleton-by-Wirksworth
Matlock, Derbyshire DE4 4LS
01629 823204

Opening hours: 9.30-5.00
(5.30 during summer)
January: closed
February-May: open weekends and school holidays
June-August: open every day
September-October: open weekends and school holidays
November-December: closed

Parsley Hay
Buxton, Derbyshire SK17 0DG
01298 84493
email: cyclehire@peakdistrict.gov.uk

Opening hours: 9.30-5.30
(or dusk if earlier)
January: closed
February: open 9-24

March-October: open
every day
November: open 1-11, 17-18,
24-25
December: closed

Waterhouses
Brown End Farm
Waterhouses
Staffordshire
ST10 3JR
01538 308313
email: greensidecottage@zetnet.co.uk

Opening hours: 9.30-6.30
(or dusk if earlier)
January-Easter: by appointment only
Easter-September: open
every day

October-December: by
appointment only

Manifold Valley
Bike Hire
Waterhouses
Staffordshire ST10 3EG
01538 308609

Opening hours: 9.30-5.30
January-February: by
appointment only
March-October: open weekends and school holidays
November-December: by
appointment only

The High Peak Trail at Middleton

Accommodation

Derby Group:

Black Horse Inn
Main Road, Hulland Ward,
Ashbourne
Derbyshire DE6 3EE
01335 370206
www.blackhorseinn-hulland.com
Rooms

Beechenhill Farm
Ilam, Ashbourne
Derbyshire, DE6 2BD
01335 310274
www.beechenhill.co.uk
Rooms

Ilam Hall Youth Hostel
Ilam Hall, Ilam
Ashbourne
Derbyshire DE6 2AZ
0870 7705876
www.yha.org.uk
Rooms

King William IV
The Bridge, Milford Belper
Derbyshire DE56 0RR
01332 842506
Rooms

The Old Vicarage
Wetton Ashbourne
Derbyshire DE6 2AF
01335 310296
www.oldvicaragewetton.co.uk
Rooms

The Old Chapel
Wetton, Ashbourne
Derbyshire DE6 2AF
01335 310450
Rooms

Matlock Bath Group:

Old Poets' Corner
1 Butts Road, Ashover, Chesterfield
Derbyshire S45 0EW
01246 590888
www.oldpoets.co.uk
Rooms and cottage
(discounts for CAMRA members)

Jug & Glass Inn, Lea
Main Road, Lea Matlock
Derbyshire DE4 5GJ
01629 534232
www.jugandglass.com
Rooms

Camping is an option in some areas of the Peak District

Temple Hotel and Restaurant
Temple Walk, Matlock Bath
Matlock, Derbyshire DE4 3PG
01629 583911
www.templehotel.co.uk
Rooms

The Nettle Inn
Hard Meadow Lane, Milltown, Ashover,
Chesterfield, Derbyshire, S45 0ES
01246 590064
Rooms

Bakewell Group:

Monsal Head Hotel
Monsal Head, Nr. Bakewell
Derbyshire DE45 1NL
01629 640250
www.monsalhead.com
Rooms

Lathkil Hotel
Over Haddon
Bakewell
Derbyshire DE45 1JE
01629 812501
Rooms

The Peacock
Rowsley, Matlock
Derbyshire, DE4 2EB
01629 733518
www.thepeacockatrowsley.com
Rooms

The Miners' Standard
Banktop, Winster
Derbyshire DE4 2DR
01629 650279
www.winster.org/miners
Camping, rooms and cottage

The Old Bakery
Church Street, Youlgrave
Derbyshire, DE45 1UR
01629 636887
Rooms and cottage

The George Hotel
Church Street, Youlgreave
Derbyshire, DE45 1VW
01629 636292
Rooms

Sheffield Group:

Stonecroft
Stonecroft, Edale, Hope Valley
Derbyshire, S33 7ZA
01433 670262
www.stonecroftguesthouse.co.uk
Rooms

Upper Booth Farm and Campsite
Edale, Hope Valley
Derbyshire
01433 670250
www.upperboothcamping.co.uk
Camping and camping barn

Little John Hotel
Station Road, Hathersage
Hope Valley
Derbyshire S32 1DD
01433 650225
Rooms and cottages

Millstone Inn
Sheffield Road, Hathersage
Derbyshire S32 1DA
01433 650258
www.millstoneinn.co.uk
Rooms

Plough Inn
Leadmill Bridge, Hathersage
Hope Valley, Derbyshire S32 1BA
01433 650319
www.theploughinn-hathersage.co.uk
Rooms

Cheshire Cheese
Edale Road, Hope Valley
Derbyshire, S33 6ZF
01433 620381
www.cheshirecheesehope.co.uk
Rooms

Huddersfield Group:

The Diggle Hotel
Station House, Diggle, Saddleworth
Lancashire, OL3 5JZ
01457 872741
Rooms

Tunnel End Inn
Tunnel End Inn, Waters Road,
Marsden, West Yorkshire HD7 6NF
01484 844636
www.tunnelendinn.com
Apartment

The Old Bridge Hotel
Market Walk, Holmfirth
West Yorkshire HD9 7DA
01484 681212
www.oldbridgehotel.com
Rooms

Buxton Group:

The Pack Horse Inn
Mellor Road, New Mills
High Peak SK22 4QQ
01663 742365
www.packhorseinn.co.uk
Rooms

Springbank
Reservoir Road
Whaley Bridge SK23 7BL
01663 732819
www.whaleyspringbank.co.uk
Rooms

Macclesfield Group:

The Church House Inn
Church Street, Bollington
Macclesfield
Cheshire, SK10 5PY
01625 574014
www.thechurchhouse-bollington.co.uk
Rooms

Heaton House Farm
Heaton House Farm
Rushton Spencer, Macclesfield
Cheshire SK11 0RD
01260 226203
www.heatonhousefarm.co.uk
Room and apartment

Hartington Group:

Alstonefield Youth Hostel
Gypsy Lane, Alstonefield,
Derbyshire, DE6 2FZ
0870 775670
www.yha.org.uk
Rooms

Barracks Farm
Beresford Dale, Hartington
Nr. Buxton, Derbyshire, SK17 0HQ
01298 84261
Camping

Charles Cotton Hotel
Market Place, Hartington
Nr. Buxton, Derbyshire
SK17 0AL
01298 84229
www.charlescotton.co.uk
Rooms

Hartington Hall Youth Hostel,
Hartington Hall, Hall Bank
Hartington
Nr. Buxton, Derbyshire
SK17 0AT
0870 7705848
www.yha.org.uk
Rooms

Dove Valley Centre
Under Whittle Farm, Sheen
Hartington, Nr. Buxton
Derbyshire SK17 0PR
01298 83282
www.dovevalleycentre.co.uk
Apartments

Stanshope Hall
Stanshope, Nr. Ashbourne
DE6 2AD
01335 310278
www.stanshope.demon.co.uk
Rooms

Leek Group:

The Black Lion Inn
Butterton, Leek
Staffordshire ST13 7SP
01538 304232
www.blacklioninn.co.uk
Rooms

Transport

Getting there:

The Peak District is well served by public transport. Driving is always an option but the towns and cities around the area are all accessible by public transport from anywhere in the UK.

Any of the cities around the Peak District would make a good base that would allow a taste of bright lights and urban culture, but if you want a more relaxed rural retreat, several of the pubs listed offer accommodation options. The accommodation index *(p146–7)* provides group-by-group listings and contact details.

National travel info:

08457 484950

www.nationalrail.co.uk

www.nationalexpress.com

Getting around:

The area enjoys a comprehensive local public transport network, although you will need either a car, careful planning or stout walking boots to reach some of the remoter areas.

Local travel info:

0871 200 22 33

www.traveline.org.uk

www.derbysbus.info

Folk trains:

In addition to regular public transport options, a number of special folk trains also run throughout the month, ferrying music lovers from the surrounding cities to Peak District pubs, whilst being serenaded by the on-board folk musicians. The trains run from Sheffield and Manchester on selected Tuesdays and Saturdays. More information can be found at www.hvhptp.org.uk.

Local train/tram operators:

Many of the walks start and end at stations, making trains a generally cheap and reliable way of accessing the Peak District.

Crosscountry Trains: www.crosscountrytrains.co.uk

East Midland Trains: www.eastmidlandstrains.co.uk

Northern Rail: www.northernrail.org

Supertram: www.supertram.net

Virgin Trains: www.virgintrains.co.uk

Local bus operators:

If you're planning to make the most of the Peak District's enviable public transport network, a copy of the *Peak District Bus Timetable* is invaluable, and available from any Tourist Information centre in the area. In addition to this, an index of the routes served by the buses recommended for the routes, is printed below.

Arriva: www.arrivabus.co.uk

First: www.firstgroup.com

Hulleys: www.hulleys-of-baslow.co.uk

Stagecoach: www.stagecoachbus.com

TM Travel: www.tmtravel.co.uk

Transpeak: www.transpeak.co.uk

Trent Barton: www.trentbarton.co.uk

BUS ROUTES INDEX

17 Stagecoach: Matlock – Chesterfield

61/62 Stagecoach: Hillsborough Interchange – Loxley – High Bradfield

64 Hulleys: Chesterfield – Matlock – Ashover – Clay Cross

65 TM Travel: Sheffield – Grindleford Mount Pleasant – Tideswell – Buxton

67 TM Travel: Chesterfield – Tideswell – Marple – Manchester

109 Arriva: Derby – Ashbourne

108 Clowes: Macclesfield – Rushton Spencer – Leek – Ashbourne

108 TM Travel: Derby – Ashbourne – Leek – Rushton Spencer – Macclesfield

113 G&J Holmes: Ashbourne – Hulland Ward – Belper

118 First: Buxton – Quarnford Travellers Rest – Leek – Hanley

171 Hulleys: Bakewell – Youlgrave – Middleton

172 Hulleys: Bakewell – Youlgrave – Birchover – Matlock

173 Hulleys: Castleton – Tideswell – Monsal Head – Bakewell

184 First: Manchester – Diggle – Huddersfield

214 Doyles: Matlock – Chatsworth – Grindleford Mount Pleasant – Sheffield

234 Clowes: Cheadle – Froghall – Ipstones – Leek

235/236 Clowes: Leek – Ipstone – Froghall – Cheadle

240 First: Sheffield – Grindleford – Bakewell

272 First: Sheffield – Hathersage – Hope – Castleton

392 Arriva: Macclesfield – Bollington – Stockport

442 Bowers: Buxton – Longnor – Hartington – Ashbourne

443 Glovers: Ashbourne – Ilam – Hartington

R1.6 Trent Barton: Derby – Belper – Wirksworth – Cromford – Rowsley – Bakewell

Transpeak: Nottingham – Cromford – Rowsley – Bakewell – Manchester

Beer styles

You can deepen your appreciation of cask ale and get to grips with the Peak's traditional beers with this run-down on the main styles available

Mild

Mild was once the most popular style of beer but was overtaken by Bitter from the 1950s. It was developed in the 18th and 19th centuries as a less aggressively bitter style of beer than porter and stout. Early Milds were much stronger that modern interpretations, which tend to fall in the 3% to 3.5% category, though there are stronger versions, such as Gale's Festival Mild and Sarah Hughes' Dark Ruby. Mild ale is usually dark brown in colour, due to the use of well-roasted malts or roasted barley, but there are paler versions, such as Banks's Original, Timothy Taylor's Golden Best and McMullen's AK. Look for rich malty aromas and flavours with hints of dark fruit, chocolate, coffee and caramel and a gentle underpinning of hop bitterness.

Old Ale

Old Ale recalls the type of beer brewed before the Industrial Revolution, stored for months or even years in unlined wooden vessels known as tuns. The beer would pick up some lactic sourness as a result of wild yeasts, lactobacilli and tannins in the wood. The result was a

Shepherd Neame's Early Bird, a Golden ale

beer dubbed 'stale' by drinkers: it was one of the components of the early, blended Porters. The style has re-emerged in recent years, due primarily to the fame of Theakston's Old Peculier, Gale's Prize Old Ale and Thomas Hardy's Ale, the last saved from oblivion by O'Hanlon's Brewery in Devon. Old Ales, contrary to expectation, do not have to be especially strong: they can be no more than 4% alcohol, though the Gale's and O'Hanlon's versions are considerably stronger. Neither do they have to be dark: Old Ale can be pale and burst with lush sappy malt, tart fruit and spicy hop notes. Darker versions will have a more profound malt character with powerful hints of roasted grain, dark fruit, polished leather and fresh tobacco. The hallmark of the style remains a lengthy period of maturation, often in bottle rather than in bulk vessels.

Bitter

Towards the end of the 19th century, brewers built large estates of tied pubs. They moved away from vatted beers stored for many months and developed 'running beers' that could be served after a few days' storage in pub cellars. Draught Mild was a 'running beer' along with a new type that was dubbed Bitter by drinkers. Bitter grew out of Pale Ale but was generally deep bronze to copper in colour due to the use of slightly darker malts such as crystal that give the beer fullness of palate. Best is a stronger version of

Mild   **Bitter**

Bitter but there is considerable crossover. Bitter falls into the 3.4% to 3.9% band, with Best Bitter 4% upwards but a number of brewers label their ordinary Bitters 'Best'. A further development of Bitter comes in the shape of Extra or Special Strong Bitters of 5% or more: familiar examples of this style include Fuller's ESB and Greene King Abbot. With ordinary Bitter, look for a spicy, peppery and grassy hop character, a powerful bitterness, tangy fruit and juicy and nutty malt. With Best and Strong Bitters, malt and fruit character will tend to dominate but hop aroma and bitterness are still crucial to the style, often achieved by 'late hopping' in the brewery or adding hops to casks as they leave for pubs.

Golden Ales

This new style of pale, well-hopped and quenching beer developed in the 1980s as independent brewers attempted to win younger drinkers from heavily-promoted lager brands. The first in the field were Exmoor Gold and Hop Back Summer Lightning, though many micros and regionals now make their versions of the style. Strengths will range from 3.5% to 5%. The hallmark will be the biscuity and juicy malt character derived from pale malts, underscored by tart citrus fruit and peppery hops, often with the addition of hints of vanilla and sweetcorn. Above all, such beers are quenching and served cool.

IPA and Pale Ale

India Pale Ale changed the face of brewing early in the 19th century. The new technologies of the Industrial Revolution enabled brewers to use pale malts to fashion beers that were genuinely golden or pale bronze in colour. First brewed in London and Burton-on-Trent for the colonial market, IPAs were strong in alcohol and high in hops: the preservative character of the hops helped keep the beers in good condition during long sea journeys. Beers with less alcohol and hops were developed for the domestic market and were known as Pale Ale. Today Pale Ale is usually a bottled version of Bitter, though historically the styles are different. Marston's Pedigree is an example of Burton Pale Ale, not Bitter, while the same brewery's Old Empire is a fascinating interpretation of a Victorian IPA. So-called IPAs with

IPA   Stout

strengths of around 3.5% are not true to style. Look for juicy malt, citrus fruit and a big spicy, peppery, bitter hop character, with strengths of 4% upwards.

Porter and Stout

Porter was a London style that turned the brewing industry upside down early in the 18th century. It was a dark brown beer that was originally a blend of brown ale, pale ale and 'stale' or well-matured ale. It acquired the name Porter as a result of its popularity among London's street-market workers. The strongest versions of Porter were known as Stout Porter, reduced over the years to simply Stout. Such vast quantities of Porter and Stout flooded into Ireland from London and Bristol that a Dublin brewer named Arthur Guinness decided to fashion his own interpretation of the style. Guinness in Dublin blended some unmalted roasted barley and in so doing produced a style known as Dry Irish Stout. Restrictions on making roasted malts in Britain during World War One led to the demise of Porter and Stout and left the market to the Irish. In recent years, smaller craft brewers in Britain have rekindled an interest in the style, though in keeping with modern drinking habits, strengths have been reduced. Look for profound dark and roasted malt character with raisin and sultana fruit, espresso or cappuccino coffee, liquorice and molasses.

With thanks to Roger Protz

Index

CAMPAIGN
FOR
REAL ALE

Books for beer lovers

CAMRA Books, the publishing arm of the Campaign for Real Ale, is the leading publisher of books on beer and pubs. Key titles include:

Good Beer Guide 2010

Editor: Roger Protz

The Good Beer Guide is the only guide you will ever need to find the right pint, in the right place, every time. It's the original and best-selling guide to around 4,500 pubs throughout the UK. Now in its 37th year, this annual publication is a comprehensive and informative guide to the best real ale pubs in the UK, researched and written exclusively by CAMRA members and fully updated every year.

£15.99   ISBN 978-1-85249-266-3

London Pub Walks

Bob Steel

A practical, pocket-sized guide enabling you to explore the English capital while never being far away from a decent pint. The book includes 30 walks around more than 180 pubs serving fine real ale, from the heart of the City and bustling West End to majestic riverside routes and the leafy Wimbledon Common. Each pub is selected for its high-quality real ale, its location and its superb architectural heritage. The walks feature more pubs than any other London pub-walk guide.

£8.99   ISBN 978-1-85249-216-8

Edinburgh Pub Walks

Bob Steel

A practical, pocket-sized travellers' guide to the pubs in and around Scotland's capital city. Featuring 25 town, park and costal walks, Edinburgh Pub Walks enables you to explore the many faces of the city, while never straying too far from a decent pint. Featuring walks in the heart of Edinburgh, as well as routes through its historic suburbs and nearby towns along the Firth of Forth, all accessible by public transport, why not stray off the Royal Mile and explore the history, architecture and landscape of the city.

£9.99   ISBN 978-1-85249-274-8

BOOKS

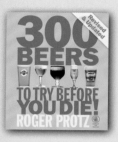

300 Beers To Try Before You Die!

Roger Protz

300 beers from around the world, handpicked by award-winning journalist, author and broadcaster Roger Protz to try before you die! A comprehensive portfolio of top beers from the smallest microbreweries in the United States to family-run British breweries and the world's largest brands. This book is indispensible for both beer novices and aficionados.

£12.99   ISBN 978-1-85249-273-1

Good Bottled Beer Guide

Jeff Evans

A pocket-sized guide for discerning drinkers looking to buy bottled real ales and enjoy a fresh glass of their favourite beers at home. The 7th edition of the Good Bottled Beer Guide is completely revised, updated and redesigned to showcase the very best bottled British real ales now being produced, and detail where they can be bought. Everything you need to know about bottled beers; tasting notes, ingre-dients, brewery details, and a glossary to help the reader understand more about them.

£12.99   ISBN 978-1-85249-262-5

Good Beer Guide Belgium

Tim Webb

The completely revised and updated 6th edition of the guide so impressive that it is acknowledged as the standard work for Belgian beer lovers, even in Belgium itself. The Good Beer Guide Belguim includes comprehensive advice on get-ting there, being there, what to eat, where to stay and how to bring beers back home. Its outline of breweries, beers and bars makes this book indispensible for both leisure and business travellers a well as for armchair drinkers looking to enjoy a selection of Belgian brews from their local beer store.

£14.99   ISBN 978-1-85249-261-8

London Heritage Pubs — An inside story

Geoff Brandwood & Jane Jephcote

The definitive guidebook to London's most unspoilt pubs. Raging from gloriously rich Victorian extravaganzas to unspoilt community street-corner locals, the pubs not only have interiors of genuine heritage value, they also have fascinating stories to tell. London Heritage pubs – An inside story is a must for anyone interested in visiting and learning about London's magnificent pubs.

£14.99   ISBN 978-1-85249-247-2

Brew Your Own British Real Ale

Graham Wheeler

The perennial favourite of home-brewers, Brew Your Own British Real Ale is a CAMRA classic. This new edition is re-written, enhanced and updated with new recipes for contemporary and award-winning beers, as well as recipes for old favourites no longer brewed commercially. Written by home-brewing authority Graham Wheeler, Brew Your Own British Real Ale includes detailed brewing instructions for both novice and more advanced home-brewers, as well as comprehensive recipes for recreating some of Britain's best loved beers at home.

£14.99   ISBN 978-1-85249-259-5

Cider

Photography by Mark Bolton

Proper cider and perry – made with apples and pears and nothing but, is a wonderful drink – but there's so much more to it than that. Cider is a lavishly illustrated celebration of real cider, and its close cousin perry, for anyone who wants to learn more about Britain's oldest drink. With features on the UK's most interesting and characterful cider and perry makers, how to make your own cider, foreign ciders, and the best places to drink cider – including unique dedicated cider houses, award-winning pubs and year-round CAMRA festivals all over the country – Cider is the essential book for any cider or perry lover.

£14.99   ISBN 978-1-85249-259-5

Order these and other CAMRA books online at
www.camra.org.uk/books,
ask at your local bookstore, or contact:
CAMRA, 230 Hatfield Road,
St Albans, AL1 4LW. Telephone 01727 867201

Find Good Beer Guide pubs on the move – anytime, anywhere!

CAMRA's two hi-tech services for beer lovers – *Good Beer Guide Mobile Edition* and the *Good Beer Guide POI* sat-nav file – offer the perfect solution to pub finding on the move.

Good Beer Guide goes mobile!

The *Good Beer Guide Mobile Edition* makes the ideal companion to the printed *Good Beer Guide*. Wherever you are, or wherever you are going, get information on local *Good Beer Guide* pubs and beers sent direct to your mobile phone.

Compatible with most mobile phones with Internet access, including the iPhone/iPod Touch, this unique service allows you to search by postcode, place name or London tube station – or it can locate your current location using GPS. Search results contain full information and descriptions for local pubs and include tasting notes for their regular beers. Interactive maps help you navigate to your destination.

To use the service, simply text **'camra'** to **07766 40 41 42**. You will then receive a text message with a web link to download the application (or, if you are an iPhone user, download the application from the App Store).

This indispensible service is **free to trial for 7 days** (excluding the iPhone/iPod Touch version) and **costs just £5** for each annual edition.

(Please note that your standard network charges apply when using this service. For more information on makes and models of phones supported, please visit: **m.camra.org.uk**)

Find *Good Beer Guide* pubs using satellite navigation!

The *Good Beer Guide POI* (Points of Interest) file allows users of TomTom, Garmin and Navman sat-nav systems to see the locations of all the 4,500-plus current *Good Beer Guide* pubs and plan routes to them. So, now, wherever you are, there is no excuse for not finding your nearest *Good Beer Guide* pub!

The file is simple to install and use and full instructions are provided. **Priced at just £5.00**, it is the perfect tool for any serious pub explorer. No more wasting time thumbing through road atlases or getting lost down country lanes. Navigate your way easily, every time, and make the most of Britain's best pubs.

To download the file visit: **www.camra.org.uk/gbgpoi**

It takes all sorts to Campaign for Real Ale

CAMRA, the Campaign for Real Ale, is an independent not-for-profit, volunteer-led consumer group. We promote good-quality real ale and pubs as well as lobbyin government to champion drinkers' rights and protect local pubs as centres of community life.

CAMRA has 110,000 members from all ages and backgrounds, brought together by a common belief in the issues that CAMRA deals with and their love of good quality British beer and cider.
For just £20 a year — that's less than a pint a month — you can join CAMRA and enjoy the following benefits:

A monthly colour newspaper informing you about beer and pub news and detailing events and beer festivals around the country.

Free or reduced entry to over 140 national, regional and local beer festivals.

Money off many of our publications including the Good Beer Guide and the Good Bottled Beer Guide.

Access to a members-only section of our national website, **www.camra.org.uk** which gives up-to-the-minute news stories and includes a special offer section with regular features.

The opportunity to campaign to save pubs under threat of closure, for pubs to be open when people want to drink and a reduction in beer duty that will help Britain's brewing industry survive.

Log onto **www.camra.org.uk** for CAMRA membership information.

**CAMPAIGN
FOR
REAL ALE**

Do you feel passionately about your pint?
Then why not join CAMRA

Just fill in the application form (or a photocopy of it) and the Direct Debit form on the next page to receive three months' membership FREE!*

If you wish to join but do not want to pay by Direct Debit, please fill in the application form below and send a cheque, payable to CAMRA, to: CAMRA, 230 Hatfield Road, St Albans, Hertfordshire, AL1 4LW. Please note than non Direct Debit payments will incur a £2 surcharge. Figures are given below.

Please tick appropriate box

	Direct Debit	**Non Direct Debit**
Single membership (UK & EU)	£20 ☐	£22 ☐
Concessionary membership (under 26 or 60 and over)	£14 ☐	£16 ☐
Joint membership	£25 ☐	£27 ☐
Concessionary joint membership	£17 ☐	£19 ☐

Life membership information is available on request.

Title_____ Surname_____

Forename(s) _____

Address_____

_____ Postcode_____

Date of Birth_____ Email address_____

Signature_____

Partner's details (for Joint Membership)

Title_____ Surname_____

Forename(s)_____

Date of Birth_____ Email address_____

CAMRA will occasionally send you e-mails related to your membership. We will also allow your local branch access to your email. If you would like to opt-out of contact from your local branch please tick here ☐ (at no point will your details be released to a third party).

Find out more about CAMRA at **www.camra.org.uk** Telephone 01727 867201

Three months free is only available the first time a member pays by DD

Instruction to your Bank or Building Society to pay by Direct Debit

 DIRECT Debit

Please fill in the form and send to: Campaign for Real Ale Ltd. 230 Hatfield Road, St. Albans, Herts. AL1 4LW

Name and full postal address of your Bank or Building Society

To The Manager _____ Bank or Building Society

Address

Postcode

Name (s) of Account Holder (s)

Bank or Building Society account number

Branch Sort Code

Reference Number

Banks and Building Societies may not accept Direct Debit Instructions for some types of account

Originator's Identification Number

| 9 | 2 | 6 | 1 | 2 | 9 |

FOR CAMRA OFFICIAL USE ONLY
This is not part of the instruction to your Bank or Building Society

Membership Number

Name

Postcode

Instruction to your Bank or Building Society
Please pay CAMRA Direct Debits from the account detailed on this Instruction subject to the safeguards assured by the Direct Debit Guarantee. I understand that this instruction may remain with CAMRA and, if so, will be passed electronically to my Bank/Building Society

Signature(s)

Date

✂ detached and retained this section

This Guarantee should be detached and retained by the payer.

The Direct Debit Guarantee

- This Guarantee is offered by all Banks and Building Societies that take part in the Direct Debit Scheme. The efficiency and security of the Scheme is monitored and protected by your own Bank or Building Society.

- If the amounts to be paid or the payment dates change CAMRA will notify you 10 working days in advance of your account being debited or as otherwise agreed.

- If an error is made by CAMRA or your Bank or Building Society, you are guaranteed a full and immediate refund from your branch of the amount paid.

- You can cancel a Direct Debit at any time by writing to your Bank or Building Society. Please also send a copy of your letter to us.